THE PRACTICE OF PRESENCE

THE PRACTICE
OF PRESENCE

Shorter Writings of
Harry Sawyerr

Edited by
John Parratt

Foreword by
Andrew Walls

WILLIAM B. EERDMANS PUBLISHING COMPANY
GRAND RAPIDS, MICHIGAN

Copyright © 1994 Board of WINDOWS ON THEOLOGY
68 Windermere Road, Lancaster LA1 3EZ

Published 1996 by
Wm. B. Eerdmans Publishing Co.
255 Jefferson Ave. S.E., Grand Rapids, Michigan 49503

Printed in the United States of America

00 99 98 97 96   7 6 5 4 3 2 1

Library of Congress Cataloging-in-Publication Data

Sawyerr, Harry.
The practice of presence: shorter writings of Harry Sawyerr /
edited by John Parratt; foreword by Andrew Walls.
p.   cm.
Includes bibliographical references.
Contents: The practice of presence — The dogma of super-size — Ancestor Worship —
The African concept of death — Psyche in conflict — What is African theology? —
The basis of a theology for Africa — Soteriology viewed from the African situation —
Christian evangelistic strategy in West Africa.
ISBN 0-8028-4115-5 (alk. paper)
1. Africa, Sub-Saharan — Religion. 2. Theology, Doctrinal — Africa, Sub-Saharan.
3. Missions — Africa, Sub-Saharan. I. Parratt, John. II. Title.
BL2462.5.S38   1995
299′.6 — dc20   95-9240
CIP

CONTENTS

EDITOR'S NOTE

Shortly before his death Harry Sawyerr handed to Andrew Walls, his former colleague at Fourah Bay College, a file of what he considered to be his most important shorter writings with a request that they should appear in book form. Several of these papers had already appeared as journal articles, others were in typescript; very few are now readily available. The editors of *Windows in Theology* are privileged to be able to fulfil the late Professor Sawyerr's wishes and make the more significant of his shorter writings available to a wider audience.

Sawyerr played a pivotal role in at least two areas of scholarship. His detailed and sympathetic research on African traditional beliefs and rituals marked him as a leading scholar in this field. Though he made extensive use of the findings of social anthropologists, his approach was essentially a religious one, exposing the theological rationale behind African spirituality with rare insight. His second great contribution was in the area of African theology, in which he was in many respects a pioneer. His article *What is African Theology?* was probably the most important single publication in the early debate about the creation of a Christian theology which would be truly African. In his continuing role in this task Sawyerr remained ever convinced of the importance of Africa's place in the long tradition of Christian thought.

Of the papers reprinted here five are representative of Sawyerr's contribution to the study of African religion. *The Practice of Presence* (originally published in *Numen* vol. XV/2 1968) is an exposition of the numinous in nature, the self and spiritual beings and demonstrates how in primal religion hierophany leads to the apprehension of the sacred and commitment to it. *The Dogma of Super Size*, which appeared in two parts in *Sierra Leone Bulletin of Religion* (vol. 4/1 1962 and vol. 5/1 1963), is an examination of the abnormal in West African religion, and focusses especially on the place of sexuality and the power of the word. *Ancestor Worship* was also first published in two parts (*Sierra Leone Bulletin of Religion* vol. 6/2 1964 and vol. 8/2 1966). Sawyerr's analysis remains very relevant to a thorny issue which continues to play an important role both in the study of African religions and African theology, and his conclusion that Africans in fact do offer worship to their ancestors is one which needs to be taken very seriously in the ongoing debate. *The African Concept of Death* (published by the WSCF, Geneva 1972) explores the meaning of death in West Africa, and leads naturally on to a discussion of the concept of 'soul'. This aspect is dealt with more fully, together with the religious rationale of sickness and healing, in the following paper *Psyche in Conflict*. I have been unable to trace any previous publication of this paper, and this text is based on Sawyerr's typescript.

The first of the articles more directly related to doing Christian theology in Africa, *What is African Theology?* was originally read at a conference organised by the All Africa Council of Churches at Mindolo, Zambia in 1970, and subsequently published in the *Africa Theological Journal* (vol. 4 1971). Sawyerr's theological methodology set out in this paper, of taking equally seriously both traditional African spirituality and the theological tradition of the ecumenical church, is well illustrated in the two papers which follow. *The Basis of a Theology for Africa* (an earlier paper which first appeared in the *International Review of Missions* vol. LII 1963) tackles the doctrines of immortality and of the omnipotence of God, while *Soteriology viewed from the African Situation* (WSCF, Nairobi 1972) explores the meaning of Christian salvation. The texts of these three papers are taken from Sawyerr's typescript and contain some minor differences from the published versions. The final piece, *Christian Evangelistic Strategy in West Africa*, was delivered to mark the centenary of the consecration of Bishop Samuel Adjayi Crowther and subsequently published in the *International Review of Missions* in 1965.

Collections of writings are inevitably often uneven and include some overlapping in the treatment of common themes. The editors are convinced, however, that the voice of Harry Sawyerr, a true 'ancestor' in the pursuit of the study of both African religions and African theology, is one which needs to be heard and heeded afresh.

We wish gratefully to acknowledge the willing cooperation and permission to reproduce this material on the part of the editors of the journals mentioned above and of the late Mrs Edith Sawyerr. We are also grateful for generous grants towards publication costs from the Pollock Trust and the SPCK.

John Parratt
Edinburgh.

FOREWORD: THE SIGNIFICANCE OF HARRY SAWYERR

Harry Aphonso Ebun Sawyerr[1] was born in the colony of Sierra Leone, on 16 October 1909. Soon afterwards his father, O'Brien Sawyerr, was sent to the recently opened station of Boma Sakrim, in Mende country in the south of the Sierra Leone Protectorate, as an agent of the Sierra Leone Church Missions, the Sierra Leone Church having taken over the Church Missionary Society's missions within the Protectorate. Boma Sakrim was his posting until 1916; he afterwards served elsewhere in the Protectorate, notably at Bo, the administrative centre, before ordination in 1922 and returning to the Freetown area on the staff of the Sierra Leone Native Pastorate, the first fruit of Henry Venn's missionary policy of self-governing, self-supporting, self-propagating churches.

His son Harry was thus brought up not only in the atmosphere of the Church, but in the midst of missonary work, of the primary encounter between the Christian faith and the old religions of Africa. He also grew into a double heritage. On one side lay the Krio Sierra Leone of the nineteenth century with its long Christian history and remarkable record of missionary enterprise beyond its borders. That tiny country ('the Colony') had appropriated the English language and British institutions; it had also developed a distinctive language and culture of its own, absorbing those Western elements into the soil of Africa. The other side of his heritage was the traditional Africa in which so much of his early life was spent. The British Protectorate which effectively fixed the borders of the modern Republic of Sierra Leone was then still new. The Mende heartland with social and religious structures resilient against change, represented a new Sierra Leone, with power to transform the old one. Harry Sawyerr was one of the people on whom fell the task of assisting the transition to a new nation which would draw from both streams. He was a 'one nation' man who united various strands in himself. Much about him was archetypically Krio; the Krio have always moved in the Western intellectual universe as proprietors, not as borrowers or squatters. And he belonged to that Krio tradition which affirmed and gloried in its African origins. He was, for instance, a vigorous champion of the Krio language (and an eloquent exponent of it) at a period when some leaders of the community denigrated it as degenerate English. 'It is full of colour and empathy, like all other African languages,' he asserted in an early foray into the media, 'and sounds African'.[2] Yet he was also deeply marked by Mendeland, and his love for and fascination with things Mende never left him. One of his earliest scholarly publications was an article on Mende grammar;[3] one of the most significant is his presentation and expansion of the collected observations of the Methodist missionary W.T. Harris, published in 1968 as *The Springs of Mende Belief and Conduct*.[4] His interest in Mende language never failed,[5] and he could combine his philological and theological concerns, as in his 'essay in detection' about the Mende name of God.[6] He also took an interest in the affairs of the Freetown Kru community with its Liberian links.[7] His sense of identity was, in fact, complex, confident and catholic; and these were qualities much needed in his time and place. Confidence in Africa, confidence in African-ness, were essential; for he grew up in a colonial setting when European paternalism was at its crudest, and in a community which was frequently the butt of European scorn. Not until a late period of his life were many in the West expecting innovatory intellectual or cultural contributions from Africa, or anything higher than creditable imitation of Western models; and he and his colleagues had long to put up with a good deal of patronage and condescension. Catholicity, readiness to appropriate the manysidedness of the African heritage, was equally important in the era of emerging nationhood when ethnic diversity could be so destructively exploited. The Krio tradition has sometimes reflected the parochialism of a small community; but its cosmopolitan origins, international dispersion and broad knowledge of the world have at other times combined to give a compelling pan-African vision, a vision of Africa's place in the world community. Harry Sawyerr had this vision.

Back in Freetown, young Harry Sawyerr attended the Prince of Wales Secondary School, showing great promise and developing a keen interest in science. At this point he came under one of the crucial influences in his life, the Freetown legend T.S. Johnson, whom in the dedication of one of his books he was to salute posthumously as 'Scholar, Teacher, Theologian, Evangelist, a Father in God and my Patron.[8]

The Rev Thomas Sylvester Johnson, later Bishop, was then Tutor at Fourah Bay College in the Theory and Practice of Education. He deserves his own footnote in the history of African theological writing. His locally published book *The Fear-Fetish: its cause and cure*[9] is a little noticed study of the tension felt by many African Christians between the elements of a world view that emanates essentially from Africa (especially what Johnson calls the 'fear-fetish') and a Christian faith which has not been integrated with that world view. Much of Harry Sawyerr's most creative future work was to be directed to that very issue, and he was to reach dimensions of the question which his mentor never glimpsed.

Johnson's immediate aim at the time of their early encounters was the recruitment of first-rate teachers, and he identified Harry Sawyerr as suitable material, encouraged him in his studies, and eventually brought him to continue those studies with himself at Fourah Bay College. Johnson's vision of education – full, rounded, undiluted – as essential to human development and Christian ministry in Africa was absorbed by his young pupil. Economic development alone would not suffice. 'We have also to develop and cultivate our minds so that we can dream dreams and see visions', the good bishop was still telling Fourah Bay students at the end of his life, and he enforced it by quoting J.E.K. Aggrey: 'Give us Science, yea, more Science, but do not give us less Greek.'[10] That is an authentic Sawyerr note too, and it is no surprise to find Sawyerr publishing this sermon of his old teacher long afterwards as a tract for the times.[11] He, too, held with passion that part of Africa's liberation lay in taking hold of the whole corpus of learning and in developing the faculties of scholarship and research. For him there were no areas or levels of study or learning which could be treated as inappropriate to Africa. He was not particularly afraid of the implicit colonialism that might arise from the form and content of Western learning. His fear was the colonialism that arose from ignorance, under-resourcing, or the patronizing judgement that certain expressions of intellectual activity desirable for the West were unnecessary for Africa. This conviction underlay his later attitude to the study of theology. Pioneer of African theology as he became, and one ever anxious to extend its applications, he saw no need to revise the received framework of the theological disciplines, and he vigorously maintained the classical approach to Biblical studies, and was wary of attempts to dismiss any particular academic activity as 'irrelevant' to Africa.

Fourah Bay, an institution unique in West Africa, claimed Harry Sawyerr's lifelong devotion and unstinting service. He joined it first as a student, took his first Arts degree there, and later received the

MA and the MEd (education was still then his primary field). He became successively tutor, lecturer, Head of the Theology department, Professor of Theology (1962), Principal (1968) and Vice-Chancellor of the University of Sierra Leone (1972). This catalogue masks not only his own, but the College's development over three and a half decades. Founded by the Church Missionary Society in 1827, it had for the succeeding century and more been West Africa's premier educational institution. Since 1876 it had been affiliated to the University of Durham, preparing students for the degrees of that University. It had attracted students from across the length and breadth of English speaking West Africa. It had produced alumni of distinction (none more so than the first on its roll, Bishop Samuel Adjai Crowther); it had been a base of serious scholarship (most notably the pioneer work of S.W. Koelle in African linguistics in the mid-nineteenth century); it had been at the centre of successive visionary strategies for Christian expansion, educational development and academic progress in West Africa. And until after the Second World War it did this from the resources of a small mission institution.[12] It is little wonder if its history is marked by recurrent failures of nerve, collapsing infrastructure and threats of closure. There were several such crises during Harry Sawyerr's association with the college; but those years also saw the most remarkable period of development in its long history.

Fourah Bay College was in those days essentially a church institution, even if theological students were a minority of the student body. It was also the apex of Sierra Leone's educational system, a monument in which Sierra Leoneans felt pride; and the link with Durham, and the presence of students from other African territories – who came because there was no such institution at home – gave it a cosmopolitan significance. This early formation lay behind the close relationship of church, education and national development which conditioned Harry Sawyerr's view of theology. Fourah Bay, even as a national university, never developed the 'Religious Studies' model pioneered by Ibadan and characteristic of African universities generally. Sawyerr's view of the place of theology in the University sometimes surprised secular minded expatriate educational experts who appeared in Sierra Leone from the 1950s. It was not based on triumphalist claims for supremacy, but on an assumption of the universal relevance of theology to all spheres of human activity, and of the responsibility of the churches to make their contribution in every sphere. It was a Johnsonian view, an expression of the attitude that had kept Fourah Bay College in being so long, and which had had frequently to contend with an alternative view, that the church should confine itself to a purely 'spiritual' sphere. Harry Sawyerr's own commitment to the church was sealed by his ordination in 1943, his activity in the community, however, was many-sided.

The Second World War brought Fourah Bay College to the brink of extinction. Its buildings were commandeered, its skeleton staff and drastically reduced student body were moved 40 miles out to Mabang; and in this state they were visited by the Elliot Commission on the post-war shape of higher education in West Africa. When the report was considered, the Secretary of State decided that Sierra Leone's modest needs for university provision could best be met at the new Nigerian university college in Ibadan.

Freetown was indignant; Sierra Leone had pioneered university education in West Africa. The community rallied to the support of its college, Protectorate voices joining with those of the Colony, and bringing financial backing which had been lacking in previous crises at the College.[13] The eventual outcome was the reconstitution of Fourah Bay College, with significant government funding and a broad-based council on a magnificent new mountain site above Freetown. The place of the churches, and especially that of CMS, in the College history was recognized, and the link with the University of Durham maintained and broadened; but Fourah Bay was now in effect, if not yet name, a university college, in parallel with its better known and better financed sisters in Ghana and Nigeria.

For some of the years of decision, Harry Sawyerr had been absent from Sierra Leone. From 1945 to 1948, accompanied by his vivacious wife Edith, he was studying theology at the University of Durham. Durham theology at the time was rigorous in the classical mode, emphatic on the importance of the Biblical languages and of the theology of the Greek and Latin fathers, and strongly Anglican in flavour. The ecclesiastical traditions of Sierra Leone were those of the evangelical CMS; in Durham Harry Sawyerr drank deeply of the Anglican Catholic stream also. It was probably an advantage that his student contemporaries were of the older, war-experienced generation. Outgoing, cheerful, interested and concerned about everything and everyone, he made abiding friendships, not least among his teachers, including Michael Ramsey, the future Archbishop of Canterbury. His attendance at the Pan African Conference in Manchester in 1945, that landmark in the history of African nationalism, is also significant.

He returned to Sierra Leone to take a responsible place in the new Fourah Bay. His primary assignment was to maintain and develop the place of academic theology in a growing institution no longer under the direction of the Church, serving the needs of an emerging nation. Close on Fourah Bay's new constitution came Sierra Leone's, the 'Stevenson Constitution' of 1951, and elections which brought Dr Milton Margai, a Mende man from the Protectorate, to be head of the government. The pattern was set for the future. Sierre Leone gained independence from Britain in 1961; in the same period Fourah Bay gained its independence from Durham, as the University College of Sierra Leone. (In 1966 came further legislation by which Fourah Bay College and the University College of Njala became parts of a federal University of Sierra Leone).

The Church to which Harry Sawyerr returned had great traditions, but perhaps a sense of being left behind in the march to nationhood. In several respects it was ill-adjusted to the new age; its ministry was ageing, and its centre of gravity lay heavily in the old colony. Sawyerr worked to reinvigorate it and to equip it to play an effective part in national life. In this project the Department of Theology had an important place. An ecumenical ministerial programme and a licence in Theology, regular vacation clergy schools, publication of a series of Aureol pamphlets were all initiatives based in the Department of Theology. In 1962 he became a Canon of St George's Cathedral, Freetown. He was perhaps too controversial a figure to become bishop; but in terms of pastoral care and concern, no one was a more devoted or time-taking shepherd, as countless students, clergy and other people can testify. The 1960s also saw him making an impact on the wider church as his stature as a theological thinker was recognized in ecumenical circles. From 1962 he was a member of the Commission Faith and Order of the World Council of Churches, and later of its working committee.

Meanwhile he was head of a department of theology which had to make its way as an academic department among other academic departments. Most of its students did not have the ministry in mind. A high proportion, as in most departments in those days, came from Nigeria, for Fourah Bay long continued to attract students from thence. Harry Sawyerr devoted his energies principally to the study and teaching of the New Testament. He developed a novel thesis about the pre-conversion background of Saul of Tarsus'[14] contributed to the debate about the framework of the Second Gospel,[15] and spent years on a major study of Pauline theology that was not published. He became a conspicuous figure at gatherings of the international (but at that time almost entirely Western) society of New Testament scholars, the Studiorum Novi Testamenti Societas. A glance at the eminent names in the New Testament field which occur in the tabula gratulantium of the Festschrift published in his honour tells its own story.

But in all this he never forgot that academic study of theology must interact with its local context; and here he made a truly pioneering contribution. He was not the first modern African constructive theologian; that place belongs perhaps to J.B. Danquah (another figure who touched African life at many points) and that remarkable book, *The Akan Doctrine of God*.[16] But Harry Sawyerr may well be the first *Church* theologian of modern anglophone Africa.[17] Others (Parrinder and Idowu among his contempories, E.W. Smith and J. Olumide Lucus among his predecessors) had explored the patterns of the primal religions of Africa, producing both studies in depth and continental surveys; Danquah had attempted to unite such studies with categories adopted from the philosophy of religion. Sawyerr bravely explored the theological implications of their work, the connexions of the old religions with Christian theology, the bridging concepts by which ideas passed in both directions.

He says that he read *The Akan Doctrine of God* at least twenty times in three years,[18] worrying away at the concept of God as ancestor mooted by Danquah. He could not leave the question where Danquah left it, a piece of detached African philosophy of religion. Nor could he ignore it; he knew that the ancestors loom too large in African consciousness to be ignored by theology. *God: Ancestor or Creator?* is an attempt to bring the concept into Christian theological discourse, by means of elements already well-rooted in the Christian tradition.

Another aspect of his thought rotated around the theme of sacrifice. Sacrifice is a theme well worked in classical Christian theology, but in a sense evacuated of much of its significance; few of its Western protagonists have ever actually *seen* a sacrifice performed. The realities of sacrifice in African life, as well as the motives for sacrifice, offer a starting point for re-examining the Biblical imagery.

In all this his pastoral concerns appear. Like Bishop Johnson with the fear-fetish, he was aware of the tensions in the minds of so many Africans between a Christian profession made with complete sincerity and elements of an African world view not assimilated to that profession. The tension was strikingly represented among his own Krio people; Christian for centuries, Christian at the very heart of their identity, and yet maintaining the ancestral rites of awujoh and developing New Year graveside libations. Harry Sawyerr studied such practices and illuminated them.[19] He also sought an-integrated Christian approach to them and to the longings and aspirations they reflected. He was completely ready to confess an envangelistic aim in his treatment of the themes of ancestors and sacrifice; they would be the basis of *creative evangelism*.[20] It is this concern which gives him a special claim to a pioneering place as a *Church* theologian.

He produced excellent students. Among pupils were later colleagues, Prince Thompson, now Bishop of Sierra Leone, and his own successors in the headship of the Department, Edward Fasholé-Luke and Leslie Shyllon. He was a genial, stimulating colleague who produced both affection and respect. *The Sierra Leone Bulletin of Religion* over the years bears witness to the activity of the Department in local research; and its expatriate members included scholars of the stature of Harold W. Turner, whose seminal and magisterial studies of African Independent Churches began within the Department and the New Testament scholar Mark Glasswell.

Harry Sawyerr's labours were never finished. When he retired from Fourah Bay he continued to serve the Church as the Principal of the Sierra Leone Theological Hall; and he left Sierra Leone only to teach in Codrington College, Barbados, which shared with Fourah Bay historic associations with the University of Durham.

He died in 1987. He has not yet been accorded his proper place in the developing story of theology in Africa, or of the theology of the Southern Continents which now produce most of the world's Christians. It is right that the richly suggestive fragments of his work presented here receive a new lease of life.

NOTES

1. The distinctively Sierra Leonean spelling of the name originated in a printing error. The brothers Moses and T.J. Sawyer opened a stationers' and booksellers' business in Freetown in 1856, becoming also the local Bible Society agents. They ordered printed bill-heads from England, which arrived containing the supernumerary 'r'. Rather than waste them, they put them to use, and accepted the consequences. C. Fyfe, *A History of Sierra Leone* (London: Oxford University Press 1962), 304.
2. *Sierra Leone Weekly News*, 30 October and 6 November 1937. On the controversy see Akintola Wyse, *The Krio of Sierra Leone: an interpretive history*, (London: Hurst 1989), 96ff.
3. 'Prepositions and post-positions in the Mende language', *Sierra Leone Studies* 1957, 209–220.
4. Freetown: Sierra Leone University Press 1968. The Rev W.T. Harris died in 1959, shortly after preparing articles on Mende marriage and inheritage law which appeared in the earliest issues of the *Sierra Leone Bulletin of Religion*, published by the Faculty of Theology at Fourah Bay College. Some years afterwards his widow made available to the Faculty the much larger manuscript which he had prepared.
5. Cf his article with S.K. Todd, 'The significance of the numbers three and four among the Mende', *Sierra Leone Studies* 26, 1972, 29–33.
6. 'Ngewo and Ngawu: an essay in detection of the origins of the Mende concept of God'; *Sierra Leone Bulletin of Religion* 9 (2) 1967, 26–33.

7. Cf his article with A.W. Sawyerr, 'Dison: a Kroo rite', *Sierra Leone Bulletin of Religion* 5(2) 1963, 47–54.
8. Dedication of *God: Ancestor or Creator?* (London: Longman 1970).
9. Freetown: The author 1949. Johnson also wrote a history of the (Anglican) Sierra Leone Church: *The Story of a Mission. The Sierra Leone Church: first daughter of CMS* (London: SPCK 1953). There is, appropriately enough, a commemoratory essay on him in the Festschrift published for Harry Sawyerr: Mateï Markwei, 'Harry Sawyerr's patron' (Bishop T.S. Johnson), in M.E. Glasswell and E.W. Fasholé-Luke (eds) *New Testament Christianity for Africa and the World. Essays in honour of Harry Sawyerr* (London: SPCK 1974), 179–197. The same work includes a bibliography of Sawyerr's writings to 1974.
10. T.S. Johnson 'New life for old: Congregation sermon preached in the College Chapel on Mount Aureol on January 20th, 1953'; *Sierra Leone Bulletin of Religion* 8 (2) 1966, 41.
11. Harry Sawyerr, at that time editor of the Bulletin, adds a note indicating the appropriateness of the sermon to the new situation, of the creation of a national university.
12. In 1953 Bishop Johnson claimed that throughout the (59) years he had been connected with the College it had never received more than £200 of Government aid in a year. (Ibid, 41, 44 n.1). From 1918 the Wesleyan Methodist (later the Methodist) Missionary Society participated in the College; subsequently the third of Sierra Leone's major churches, and the largest in the Protectorate, the Evangelical United Brethren (since joined with the American Methodists in the United Methodist Church) also joined.
13. T.S. Johnson, *Story of a Mission*, 103ff.
14. 'Was St Paul a Jewish missionary?'', *Church Quarterly Review* 1959, 457–463.
15. 'The Markan framework', *Scottish Journal of Theology*, 14(3) 1961, 279–294.
16. London: Lutterworth Press 1944.
17. There were stirrings in Franchophone Africa among Roman Catholic writers; there is no clear sign of these influences in Sawyerr's work, though he early read Janheinz Jahn's *Muntu* (1961).
18. *God: Ancestor or Creator?* x.
19. Cf of many, 'Graveside libations in and near Freetown', *Sierra Leone Bulletin of Religion* 7 (2) 1965, 48–55; 'More graveside libations in and around Freetown', *Sierra Leone Bulletin of Religion* 8 (2) 1966, 57–59; 'A Sunday graveside libation in Freetown, after a bereavement', *Sierra Leone Bulletin of Religion* 9 (2) 1967, 41–45.
20. The title of his first book (London: Lutterworth Press 1968).

Andrew Walls
Edinburgh

THE PRACTICE OF PRESENCE

A Discussion of Some of the Factors which Make up the
Apprehension of the Supernatural with Special Reference
to West Africa

1. INTRODUCTION

To pre-scientific man, Nature is a medley of presences. The blaze of
a flash of sheet-lightning, the frightening din of a thunder-clap, the
destruction wreaked by winds of gale-force; or the sudden encounter
in a forest, of a menacing serpent or of a beast of prey e.g. a lion or
a tiger, or the sudden darkness that obscures a bright moonlight
during a lunar eclipse; the change that comes on a man of stalwart
physique as a result of sickness, and his subsequent death, all give
the impression of a presence or presences within Nature. So too the
unusual behaviour of the night-jar, the bat and the owl – birds which
go out at night when other birds have gone to roost – strike pre-
scientific man as possessing special qualities which suggest their
possession of special powers, attributable to a presence. Similar ideas
are held of trees which are hard to cut and of stones and rocks of
peculiar shapes and sizes. In short, man at this stage, attributes
presences to the factors which constitute his environment. These
presences therefore make up reality for him. These contrasts and
contradictions of life are however not limited to early man. In the
language of John Baillie, 'Reality is what I come up against, what
takes me by surprise, the other-than-myself which pulls me up and
obliges me to reckon with it and adjust myself to it because it will
not consent simply to adjust itself to me.'[1] 'For most of the time,
reality shows itself in its concealments.'[2] It cannot therefore be
apprehended by finite minds, however intelligent they may be. This
experience of being confronted by a something, one cannot fully
interpret leads to the awareness of the Other, the Thou, I would
prefer the Him. Conative and emotional factors are thus evoked in
the individual, and his behaviour is accordingly determined by them.
A discussion of the *Practice of Presence* in West Africa is therefore

1

essentially an attempt to examine some of the ways in which, early man and the West African, in particular, essayed to interpret and to deal with the factors of his environment which confronted him.

2. EARLY MAN AND HIS ENVIRONMENT

Early man did not make any analytical distinction between himself and his environment. For early man, reality was a single whole. He felt himself part of the whole environment around him. Indeed, he did not distinguish between the various parts of his body and their several functions, on the one hand, and the totality of his existence, on the other. Thus, for example, as in almost all Africa, a man's person was thought to be exposed to danger, if the clippings of his hair, the parings of his finger nails, the footmarks that he left behind or his clothes were to come within the reach of an enemy. He also kept his name dark to a stranger for the same reason. Indeed, up to less than fifty years ago, barbers were not popular in Freetown. Hair-cutting was done at home, and the clippings were carefully collected afterwards. It used also to be said that if the fire-finch, a reddish coloured bird which hopped around houses with a sense of security, should pick up the clippings to make its nest warm, the person from whose head they had been cut out would go mad.

One feature of this attitude which is related to the present study is the tendency in West Africa to attribute human qualities to animals and inanimate objects. So the Akan regard the bat as a diplomat; to the Yoruba, vultures are embodied manifestations of the dead who always flock to places where family sacrificial rites are performed in honour of the dead, although in fact they are attracted by the carrion. So too, the chameleon is a messenger of *Olodumare*, the Yoruba God. A Limba story which in all respects is a version of the story of Adam and Eve, resolves the temptation in the garden of Eden by the explicit remark that the serpent made love with Eve (*Ifu* in the story).[3] The Temme of Sierra Leone believe that the spider is capable of detective powers and embodies cunning and astuteness, because of its capacity to propel itself along a strand of its thin web. This anthropomorphism is noticeable in the stories which are told among the West African tribes. Trees and stones are also believed to have power and excellence which is usually expressed in terms of spirits, conceived as human beings, residing in them. The more unusual the

2

stone or the tree, the more powerful it became to pre-scientific man. So the Akan attribute a fierce spirit, (*sunsum*), to the *tweneboa* tree, an African cedar (?), because it resists cutting and therefore, when felled, provides a log which could be deeply excavated to a thin layer which produces a high resonance, when fitted with a skin membrane to make a drum. (This is the wood used for making the *ntumpane* or talking drums). Because of the potential resistibility of this wood, the Akan appease the spirit with eggs and rum, before felling it, and, again, before excavating it into the hollow cylinder over which the skin membrane is stretched. They however later invite the spirit to return to the hollow wood as to its original habitat.[4] The darkness caused by a lunar eclipse, especially when it is total, is attributed to either a spirit which attacked the moon, (so the *Mende*), or to a struggle between the sun and the moon (so the *Yoruba*). But perhaps even more so powerful, are the features of the thick forests, the grasses and savannahs of the tropics – the habitat of prowling spirits; so when a man loses his way in a forest and often never returns or is found distraught and exhausted after an intense search, he is said to have been the victim of a huge forest monster. The Akan of Ghana call him *sasabonsam*, which they say, sits in the branches of trees dangling his legs, in wait for a lone traveller. The Mende of Sierra Leone talk of a hairy man called *D'gb'joso*, (forest-wizard), who is also referred to by the Temnes and Sierra Leone Creoles as *ronsho*. In every case it is held that he compels travellers to travel far into the forest and so become liable to perish as a result of exhaustion. Again, some men perhaps in a state of emotional instability, are said to encounter in cleared patches bordering a farm or within a forest, little men (Akan, *mmoatia*, Mende, *tenui*), which possess oracular powers and teach them the medicinal value of certain herbs.[5] Even birds fluttering in the forest and calling, to one another, perhaps in their mating season, are suggestive of spirits accompanying the travellers who hear them.

This is true of the Mende, *Bofio*. So a Mende traveller who hears the cry of the *Bofio* always makes an offering of something he is carrying – a piece of leaf tobacco or some food – which he lays along the road-side, saying at the same time, 'Cease calling, here is a present for you'! River-spirits are postulated chiefly to explain rapids, and whirlpools, or to account for the foam that is created when a river rushes past a huge rock jutting above its surface, or when frail craft founder on a like rock before the river has been adequately charted. To the West African then, nature is full of power, power like man's but often hostile to him. We may go on to say then that long before man practised agriculture he had come to realize that the discovery of fire was a key achievement for his life and work. Fire burns and destroys much of the environment. It is said to be most feared and, perhaps, the single dangerous enemy of the reptile world. But fire burns man. The *Kposso* myth on the origin of leprosy suggests that primitive man was not himself left unscathed by his invention.[6]

Again, pre-scientific man is afraid of sickness and death. The Temne of Sierra Leone personalise sickness as an old man and death as a man in the vigour of youth sent down to the world by the Supreme Deity. So sickness and death are thought of as messengers of God.[7] The *Kposso* too believe that mankind suffers from leprosy because a bird whom God produced out of fire, beat a man, *Sropa*, who disobeyed God's orders not to warm himself by means of fire.

This is the basis of mythical thought by which man began to invent explanations of his experiences. At the beginning, man was part of the totality of his environment. With the apprehension of power, man began to distinguish between himself and the constituent elements of his environment. So in West Africa, there has developed a whole catalogue of spirits to explain the basis of world-order. The World is full of spirits, ranged around a supreme spirit, the Deity, God. animals, trees and stones have souls, or at least are inhabited by spirits, some of which are naturally hostile to man or become so when angered. To the Supreme Deity is attributed the creation of the physical and spiritual forces in the world; the Earth itself is a spirit and, sometimes a goddess: in some areas, she is the wife of the Supreme Deity. Just as seminal fluid waters the body of a woman, thereby causing her to bring forth children, so rain, falling on the earth from the sky, produces vegetation. Where, as in the case of the Akan, the Supreme Deity was earlier conceived as a Lunar Mother-goddess, the Earth was thought of as her daughter – with a double aspect, the one producing vegetation, (*Asaase Afua*), and, the other, identified with barrenness and death, (*Asaase Yaa*). The consequential rivers that flow along the surface of the earth were also thought by the Akan to be gods e.g. River *Tano* whose progeny is legion, all of them gods. Accordingly, to the Akan, water *per se* possesses a power which it loses when boiled. Boiled water is therefore used only for washing corpses but never an infant.[8] Among the Mendi, in Sierra Leone, the Earth is ŋgew'nyahɛi, maand", Mother Earth, ŋgew"s wife or sometimes *Maaŋgew'*, Mrs. ŋgew', and so, Mother God, where ŋgew' is a male deity.

The Earth is in any case, a power. All vegetable life-forms sprout forth from it; the dead lie buried in it and their influence on man, for better or for worse is associated with it. We shall consider the ancestral dead later. Vegetable life, however, suggests the origins of human life and so babies are believed to take their origin from the earth.

The reality of life is thus conceived as an encounter between man and other spirit-influences which are generally different from and in some cases resistant to man. They are all regarded as being more powerful than man.

So there develops a concept of Power as an aspect of Presence. God is the great Power and the rest of creation constitute, in essence, the manifestation, in large or small measure, of Power. Presence has now assumed the dimension of Power, residing in some object – man and objects other than man.[9]

3. MAN'S DISCOVERY OF HIMSELF

The most concrete instance of Presence is however, man, himself. His own body is a Presence. A child learns to discover the various parts of his body – his nose, his mouth, his forehead, his toes, his ankles, his ears, his eyes, his hair, and so on. No doubt he had already used them as instruments of smelling, eating, seeing, hearing, holding and gripping since he was a few weeks old. But he only apprehends the fact of their existence when the child discovers them as separate parts of his body. The way a baby, say, 18 months old, comes to experience water running from a tap flowing on, and through his fingers is truly illuminating. In spite of mother's rebukes, I have been fascinated by the way infants in their second year of life have refused to let me turn a tap off when, after having washed their hands, they let the water trickle through their fingers. I admit this is an experience into which I can not now fully enter. But after watching several generations of children, I believe I can safely infer what it is. Their behaviour has left me with the impression always that it thrills them to perform this exercise. I have myself tried to reconstruct their experiences by letting water run through my fingers from a tap and have been led to the conclusion that the experience is at two levels:

First, one becomes sensitive to the presence of the water because of its coldness; secondly, the separate fingers acquire an individuality as the cold water produces a feeling of numbness in each finger. Each finger now feels different from the other. For an infant, this awareness constitutes a real discovery. To this discovery we may add the well known tendency for children not only to acquire invisible playmates at the age of four but also to treat the flowers and plants around their home as imaginary human beings. They talk to them, sometimes in ways repetitive of their own experiences with the members of their family. These illustrations are, in fact, indicative of the experience of primitive man. He projects himself into his environment and so postulates the spirits to which we referred earlier.

In short, then, Reality becomes cognizable with the discovery of man by early man, a discovery which, as has been said already, leads to the distinction between the first and second or third person, I and Thou or, preferably, Him.

At this stage, man develops two contradictory attitudes. He sees in the inanimate objects all round him, instances of the human capacities he has discovered in himself, and so develops the attitude described by Levy-Bruhl as the Law of Participation.[10] At the same time, he tends to feel himself at their mercy. Inanimate objects have Power like man's Yes! but the power of the (Akan) *tweneboa* tree seems to be greater than man's. The *Olum'*, Rock of Abeokuta in Nigeria, towers high above the ground as one solid ball, but in fact it encloses cavities which can shelter several hundred men and did on one occasion save them from utter destruction. Man therefore begins to attribute Power to the inanimate objects of his perception, and so begins to draw a distinction between himself and them. But are the percepts, reflections of man's image of himself or are they the criterion on which he develops his own self-consciousness? In West Africa, the Akan believed that the sun that sets on one evening dies and another comes up on the next day. Equally, to the Yoruba of Nigeria a lunar eclipse is the result of a struggle between the sun and the moon; to the Mende of Sierra Leone, the struggle takes place between the moon and some celestial spiritual being, (*nyaŋguma*). What then is the basis on which this kind of reasoning is worked out? Is the death of the sun postulated in terms of man's death and total disappearance? The Akan answer is in terms of a postulated deity, *Odomankoma* who is said to have made death eat poison, when death killed him. Is the lunar eclipse suggestive of man's experience of obstacles which thwart his progress? Or is the resulting darkness a symbol of death to all mankind a factor of special significance to a migratory tribe? Man is thus led first to believe that Nature is a powerful agent; later fear and a sense of helplessness creates in him the sense of the numinous, with its twin contrary components – the *mysterium tremendum et fascinans*.[11] But he first resists and seeks to control the forces which constitute his environment, by devising a power which he postulates can subdue them. This is magic. The factors of life however remain unbending and so he surrenders and

6

later subordinates himself to the numinous. He then establishes a code of ethical behaviour that would establish a full rapport with the deity he serves. This is religion. The discovery of the numinous is a hierophany which leads to an apprehension of the sacred.

We refer to this experience as an I and Thou or Him-relationship by which we mean that the I attributes to the Thou or Him-factor the form of activity that it attributes to itself. This attitude explains 'the animism both of young children and of primitive man.'[12] In other words, we would say that at the lowest stages of human existence there exists, on the one hand, a mythical concept of the soul, and so of projected psychic factors in things material and, on the other, the manifestation of demonic power to which he is likely to succumb. We now find a bond created between the I and the Thou or Him through which contrary situations of a definite unity and a definite contrast; a relation of kinship and a relation of tension are created between the individual and his environment. These relationships form the bases of *totems* and their correlative *taboos*. Man now finds himself in a position in which his ideals assume psychic form embodied in physical entities which become alien to himself. As a result, demonic powers dominate the individual's experience. Indeed, even his own soul, tends to assume demonic proportions.[13] So, as among the Yoruba, the belief prevails that everyone is born with a fixed destiny, *Ori*, the personality soul, (literally, a head). But the term also implies a man's future destiny, granted him by the Supreme Deity, Ɔlɔrun. Again, an individual may also look like an embodiment of his grandfather's spirit, *Ori* may then connote a spiritual double, a guardian angel with which the individual has to live harmoniously. A man who violates his *Ori* may then either fall ill or, meet with bad success in his profession.[14] Here the *Akan* concept of *kra* and *sunsum* is also significant. Everyone has a spark of deity, his *kra* which is the vital principle of blood, coming down from the supreme deity, at first *Nyame*, but later *Nyankopon*, as well as a personality-soul, *sunsum*, originally associated with *Odomankoma*, which according to the later assumptions, he derives from his father. The *kra* and the *sunsum* are however often said to be liable to struggle, each with the other when the *sunsum* is not attuned to the demands of the *kra*. In such a case, the disharmony leads to physical illness. At the same time protection from evil attacks, e.g. of witches, is attributed to the *kra*. A similar concept is embodied in the Tallensi *Ehi*, the local word for fate and destiny.[15] In this context the individual's voice, as representative of his soul can be either a supporting influence, as when a blessing is uttered, or a destroying agent, as when a curse is uttered, the latter phenomenon being a demonic expression of the spiritual power inherent in the individual.

This demonic aspect of the soul is best noticed at the communal level where it performs the functions of conscience. Ontologically, conscience in this context, represents a *communis sensus*, built up in the individual by informal education from early childhood as a result of which an inbuilt resistance to wrong-doing, private or public, is first established, and then maintained through appropriate practical instruction on the dangers which would result from any violation of the several sanctions. Thus, among the Mende of Sierra Leone, although no one may know that a man or woman has commited incest, yet he falls ill and so has to go first to a diviner, who directs him to a *Hum'i* priest. He is then brought to the cultic shrine where he makes a full and open confession of his actions, offers a sacrifice, is ritually washed, pays a fine and returns home with confident hope of a speedy recovery. Again, among the *Mende* we have the very interesting situation where when a man plants a cassava farm, he usually places a guardian medicine in it to ward off thieves and often, witches also. The invocation of this guardian medicine always includes however a venial clause which allows for a long-distance traveller or anyone who is genuinely hungry to pluck up a root of cassava and eat enough to satisfy his hunger, provided he does not remove any for later use. The result is that we find two men, the one, on a long-distance journey or genuinely hungry, and the other, a thief, both plucking roots of cassava from someone else's farm. The traveller or genuinely hungry person, if he keeps to the rules, will feel no ill after-effects. The thief will fall ill and later develop a compulsion for confessing his theft to a native-doctor to whom he would have been directed by a diviner. He then has to go through a religious rite, followed by an act of restitution, before he recovers.

Here then we see how pre-scientific man reacts to his environment both by efforts to control it as well as by sheer submission to it. In both cases the I is fully involved. As we have already noted, these two features are the result of the discovery of the Thou or Him and also of the later apprehension of the I as an ethical subject. A basic ingredient in this development is the role of desire – human desire. The two illustrations taken from among the Mende, mentioned above are typical. In general, judging from the prayers uttered as sacrificial rites, the petitions are chiefly in regard to rain, fruitful harvests, the fertility of the women, health to the babies and strength and success to the men.[16] We would therefore suggest that desire constitutes the fount of the religious consciousness, i.e. that sense of the presence of the unseen which creates in man a sense of values, especially of good and evil, of right and wrong. My understanding of tribal life leads me to the view that whilst the various creation-myths always

8

tend to postulate a primal couple, sometimes just a single man, man, however, only becomes aware of himself in the double context of I and Thou or Him,

(a) with respect to his fellow-man
and (b) with respect to the material objects around him.[17]

In a Temme myth recorded by Schlenker, the latter relationship seems to come first.[18] But the human situations always seem to be reproduced in nature, in other recorded myths. Thus, the I – Thou or Him relationships present a double problem:

(i) The postulation of divine destiny granted to the individual before the soul enters the body. He may choose his destiny or it may be conferred on Him by the supreme Deity at a leave-taking ceremony, before his birth. This notion raises questions of creationism which call for further investigation; it certainly forms an integral factor in primitive mythical reasoning.

(ii) The recognition of the existence of human characteristics inherited from one's physical parents, and earlier forbears. So although the *Akan kra* is a divine spark, yet the *sunsum*, later identified with the *ntorɔ* is understood to be inherited from the father, and the father's *ntorɔ* god associated with water – chiefly an expanse of water. At the other end of the scale, we find the Mende of Sierra Leone believe that a man inherits his spirit *ŋgafa*, from his mother, and his blood, flesh and bones from his father. At the same time, since the Earth is often described on solemn occasions as Mother-God* and more frequently so as Mrs *ŋgewɔ* as in the invocation, 'You and Your wife, Mother Earth', there does seem to exist an implicit belief among the Mende that everybody is

(a) supposed to have originated from the Earth and so
(b) has a divine spark, even if not directly acquired from the Supreme Being.

It seems justified to suggest, therefore, that the processes of human pro-creation are implied in the assumption that the Earth is the Mother of mankind, with *ŋgewɔ* in the sky as the ultimate Father. She is *maand*, Mother-Earth.

In some cases, these two aspects overlap as in the case of the Yoruba, *Ori*. Man is thus a combination of two presences – the one supernatural, derived from the supreme God. I shall call this presence *theomorphic*; the other, *genetic*, derived from one's human predecessors

---

* In a sense similar to Mother Hubbard, i.e. a woman with a large family.

9

which I shall call *patri* – or, as in the case of the Mende, *matri* – *morphic*. Two new factors now emerge:

  (i) the community with special reference to the ancestors,
and (ii) the Supreme God and various tutelary deities including the
      Earth.

We are now in the sphere of religion – the core of tribal life.

4. RELIGION AND COMMUNAL TRIBAL LIFE

Tribalism is thus usually described in language which presents it as resistant to change and therefore not attuned to the contemporary situation. This study is however concerned, primarily, with the role of religion in tribal life. Tribal life is, however, through and through, religious. The society is maintained by its religious outlook. At the same time, 'the true object of religion, the sole and original object to which all religious forms and expressions can be traced back, is the social group to which the individual indissolubly belongs'. Tribal man more than any other is always made aware by the structure of his society that he is a link in a chain of life, which consists of the whole society; a chain preserved by the religious rites and observances of the community. An interesting example of this attitude is seen when a curse is laid among the Mende of Sierra Leone, in relation to a case of theft. The theft is reported to the chief and the intention of the victim to lay a curse (*sondu*), usually wrongly translated *swear*, is made known to the chief of the town or village. The˚medicine to be used is declared and a token fee paid to him for permission to perform the rite on a requested site. When this permission has been obtained, public notification both of the theft and the intention to lay the curse is made around the village, in some cases by an official town-crier, on three successive nights, i.e. at times when everbody is supposed to be back home after the day's work on the farm. Then the whole village is summoned to the site where the curse is to be laid. The theft is once more reported, the attendant circumstance consequent to the curse is described, and the curse laid. The onlookers thus give their approval, as a community, to the act.

But the offender is not the only person mentioned. All his relations, anyone with whom he may have shared the stolen article, especially so if it was food; any friend closely associated with him; in short, anyone, who may know or be even vaguely aware of the possible identity of the culprit, comes under the curse. In that way,

10

information is often released, or someone comes forward to stand in for a supposed suspect and makes restitution to the victim for his loss and the expenses he has incurred in connection with all the preparations for laying the curse. This sense of corporateness is manifested in other areas where the socio-moral code has been violated. Thus in one version of the *Hum'i* cult among the Mende, the close relations of a person guilty of incest, who are within easy reach are all brought together and castigated as part of the cleansing ceremony by which the penitent is restored to normal societary privileges. So too when a young Mende man invokes the curse of a maternal uncle for disloyalty often through refusal to obey his behests, all his brothers and sisters are required to take part in a ceremony at which they are each personally forgiven for the disobedience of the offending brother. A collective dimension is obviously attributed to the cases we have been describing.

But this attitude does not mean the total obscurity of the individual. His personal claims are respected and his personal dignity maintained. Thus among the Mende of Sierra Leone, a man who had, say, several men in his employ, or, in the old days, owned many slaves, was expected to treat them all with comparable fairness and impartiality. If he failed to do so, the aggrieved servant could invoke *hakε*, a curse associated with bad human relationships. It is believed that *hakε* has the peculiar character of being able to pursue an offender even after his death. *Hakε* is obviously a demonic presence which can only be revoked by a religious sacrificial rite. This close inter-action of religious attitudes and social behaviour influences every aspect of tribal life and determines customary behaviour.

5. WITCH-CRAFT

At this stage we must make a brief reference to the belief in witchcraft, particularly so that type which is said to be able to leave the body when the witch is asleep and goes out to attack another person, infant or adult, when he is also asleep. We would here suggest that the belief is an expression of the disapproval of a breach of world-order. (As could be inferred already, tribal life is strictly traditional and does not readily admit of any violations of the accepted order. Tribal society therefore frowns on any departure from the norm). Since this form of witchcraft is associated with the destruction of life, in societies like those of the Yoruba or Mende, for example, witches are usually women. On close examination, witchcraft is associated with women who are queer, who are past child-bearing and indeed disinterested in, even if not resistant to, male associations; who are hostile to children; who are cruel, often tending to be sadistic; or who are callous and capable of revolting behaviour not thought to be compatible with the accepted gentility associated with motherhood, and lady-like elegance and dignity.

Here again is a presence which tends to destroy life and does not contribute to the well-being of the community. In this context, it is remarkable that incestuous practices and witchcraft are said by Radcliffe-Brown to be closely associated. He goes on to say 'There is a widespread belief in Africa that a man can obtain the greatest power as a sorcerer by incestuous intercourse with his mother or his sister'.[19] It is thus not surprising that Laubscher writing of the Tembu of South Africa remarks that 'The native's attitude and reactions towards witchcraft have some analogy to the thinking and acting of the compulsive neurotic patient. Both are struggling against the dynamic expressions of forbidden impulses. The obsessional neurotic is defending himself from the world of mythical beings'.[20] Laubscher is obviously thinking of two mythical beings: First, the *Tikoloshe*, a mythical dwarfish man with a *huge penis*, often mentioned by the Tembu women, as having 'great knowledge of witchcraft . . . and is frequently named as the vehicle by means of which other persons exercise witchcraft'. He is at the same time said to be 'known to put himself at the disposal of those wishing to counteract witchcraft'.[21] Secondly, the *Impundulu*, a bird 'with beautifully and highly-prized feathers', which is supposed to be 'a powerful carrier of witchcraft.' It is believed to be sadistic and 'to cohabit quite regularly with witches'; and is described as having a penis said to be 'long, thick and flat and about the size and appearance of an ox-tongue.'[22] Alastair Scobie, writing of the Transvaal, also relates how young women of that country enjoyed copulation with baboons. They are therefore branded as witches and are said to acquire by such an act a familiar, often described as a cross between a human being and a baboon, but more often as a dwarf.[23]

These instances of witchcraft emphasize an aspect often little recognised. Significant, therefore, as Marjorie Field's analysis of witchcraft in Ghana is, one cannot help concluding, however, that her diagnosis of witchcraft in terms of anxiety and depression is limited and primarily suits the patient who assumes that he or she is a victim of witchcraft. We yet have to explain this belief not only in terms of the condition and attitude of the victim but in the wider context of those who accuse others of acts of witchcraft and the correlative universal dread of the spirits of witches. In this context, Chief Anthony Enahoro's claim that better health and education reduces the belief in witchcraft is not supported by most of those who have gone seriously into the problem.[24] I suggest therefore that basic to witchcraft is the question 'why'? to sadism. In the African situation, sadism and the postulation of witchcraft seem generally to go together. Sadism, in West Africa, is therefore the manifestation of a presence which is hostile to the well-being of communal life and is therefore condemned publicly. It has demonic overtones. So the owl, predatory animals which destroy food-crop harvests at night, any pest infestations which destroy stocks of food – rats, termites, for example – the kr-kr-kr-r-r-r of the vampire bat are physical manifestations of witches in action. The vampire bat sucks the blood of babies and so leaves them lame in one or both limbs.

6.   WE LIVE WITH OUR DEAD[25]

However strong and influential the factors that affect the relationships of the living may be, perhaps, the most important social bond is that of the relation of the living members of a tribe or clan or family to their ancestral dead. Not all the dead are regarded as of ancestor-class. This is true of babies and in some areas of adults who die childless, (in particular, without a male child). In addition, the spirits of those who either met with a violent death, or who were denounced as witches, or who were believed to have died prematurely are said to be outside the acknowledged abode of the dead. Thus there are the so-called wandering spirits – the *Saman-twentwen* of the Akan, and the *pelehunga-yafɛisia* of the Mende, to quote two examples. Of course the spirits of witches are, as far as one can judge, not allowed to survive – the corpses of witches are either burnt (the Efik), dismembered (the Temne), thrown in swamps (the Kalabari), or buried in a shallow grave (the Mende). In general, however, the dead were usually buried in or around their homes as among the Mende of Sierra Leone for example. But even though dead, the ancestors play an ambivalent role. First, they are believed to continue to exist in their descendants by re-incarnation. Indeed, even before he dies, an Akan grandfather would spit into the mouth of his grandson at the out-dooring ceremony in order to strengthen his *sunsum* or *ntorɔ* already passed on, perhaps in a diluted form, through his son, the father of the infant. When a child is born soon after the death of either of the husband's parents, the Yoruba call him *Babatunde* or *Iyatunde*, if a girl, i.e. 'father or mother has come back'. The Akan believe that the souls of their deceased are re-incarnated in the family to enable them to attain their original

13

destiny. Of course, this notion is based on a fractional interpretation of re-incarnation, because the spirit of a deceased person could at the same time be invoked at his grave-side. Most West Africans adopt this theory of re-incarnation to explain the genetic factors which are present in the procreative process. We recall what had been said earlier of the Yoruba *Ori*, viz: that the term may mean, grandfather's spirit, and at the same time, one's double. In short, they assume that the ancestors live close to their descendants or are, at least, of ready access to them. Secondly, the ancestors exercise juridical and economic authority over their descendants. It is remarkable that in Sierra Leone, and indeed in the capital, Freetown, the ancestral rites are always occasions of family re-unions and of settling inter-family disputes. The assumed authoritative presence of the ancestors makes it imperative that their descendants, present or absent, are of one accord. This attitude is quite marked among the westernised and Christianised Creoles of Freetown. The authority once wielded by the ancestral dead during their life-time in the maintenance of good moral standards is always assumed to be implicitly predominant.[26] Among the *Mende* of Sierra Leone, the invocations at a national festival begin from the oldest remembered dead to the latest, before reference is made to the generality of forbears no longer remembered individually. They are the apical factors of the life of the nation, the tribe, the clan and the family. The ancestral spirits are in general well-disposed towards the members of their families. Of course, they could get angry and vengeful. It is therefore desirable both to maintain the family ties intact. Close as well as distant relatives are therefore all, alike, under a moral obligation to contribute towards the funeral rites of members of the family, whether nuclear or extended. When a relative cannot participate at an actual funeral, other opportunities are provided e.g. second burials among the Yoruba, or festivities to mark seventh and fortieth days or anniversaries. A respected, and therefore good member of the family must however go into the spirit world endued with goodness. The Mende of Sierra Leone therefore ensure that the spirit of an otherwise good person does not meet with any misfortunes, caused by a vengeful attitude of anyone he might have offended. They have therefore devised a rite, *Kpila gbualɛi*, (removing the grounds for complaints), at which all, who bear him a grudge, come forward and state their grievances and all, to whom he is indebted, state their claims for payments due them, before he is buried. A senior member of the family of the deceased then stands surety, sometimes nominally, for the debts. After all the grievances have been declared, and the payment of just debts is ensured,

14

everybody present, one by one, declares, '*hakε i lo*,' i.e. 'May the (avenging) curse (*hakε*) which would have followed him in the other world because of the grievances we held against him be stayed'!

7. CONCLUSION

In a brief study of some of the factors which constitute Presence, in the West African situation, we recall that the individual begins by identifying himself with the animate and inanimate elements of Nature. Later, he comes to distinguish himself from them, through the frustration that comes of being thwarted by some superior physical force to which he attributes psychical essence. He however comes to find that there is yet a sub-division or sub-divisions within himself, all of which he first tends to assume are replicas of his total individual personality. So his voice, his shadow, the clippings of his hair, the parings of his nails are all segmented parts of his person, all of which are endowed with power. Some of these may be directed outwards, away from him, as when he utters a blessing or a curse; or they may turn against him with demonic violence as is the case of the in-built mechanism which compels a man with an uneasy conscience – usually when he feels himself the victim of a curse – to confess a crime which had not been hitherto detected.

Man's concept of himself thus develops a bi-polar content, the one, a guardian angel, well disposed towards him and the other, a hostile demonic force, alien to him. In this context, desire, becomes an important and dominant factor. Values, accordingly emerge which take their origin from a *communis sensus* derived from the community to which the individual belongs. So the I having first discovered the Thou or Him of his environment, subsequently classifies this into a Thou or Him of the other person as well as a Thou or Him of material objects he regards as possessing psychic qualities. Later, he himself plays the double role of an I and a Thou with relation to himself. The last Thou being in fact the self as object and the I, the self as subject.

When the I arrives at the stage where it can be both subject and object, man has also come to taste of experience. But is all experience of the subject-object type? We are reminded of Professor I.T. Ramsey's references to 'odd-discernment.'[27] We also recall the earlier remark that reality is a confrontation, one rich instance of which, we then noted, led to the discovery of persons. Even the discovery of the self is an odd-discernment. Out of these odd situations there always seems to emerge the recognition of something

15

to which man feels himself committed. Primitive man sees this, first, in his use of tools and in the invention of fire. Thus among the *Mende* of Sierra Leone, farmers always look for a good whetstone on any land they intend to cultivate. If they find a suitable one they keep it for several generations within the same family. Sometimes neighbouring farmers ask to use it. After a given period of varying duration, the stone becomes sacred to its users and is sometimes used to lay a curse. It is believed that the guilty person would see, in a dream, a man in a yellow gown when such a curse had been laid, and that this man is the personification of the power that resides in the stone. The odd-discernment of a given piece of rock as a good whetstone has moved on to an odd-commitment by which the whetstone is preserved by the family and the apprehension of a being of transcendence identified with it. Man has at last reached a stage at which the unseen has an impelling call. He is on the quest for the divine, but he only has concrete material factors available. So he moves in two planes. He creates minor deities or 'fetishes' of an ever increasing number. For example, it is said that the Yoruba have 401 such divinities on a conservative estimate; but, as Professor Idowu suggests, there may easily be 1700 of them.[28] The shrine of *Orisa-nla* at Ife is surrounded by hundreds of little shrines representing various grades of the ministers of Olodumare. These minor deities provide the answer to man's immediate needs. Some offer supernatural help to the hunter e.g. the Yoruba *Ogun*; others represent energy, e.g. of lightning (Yoruba, *Shango*); yet others still prosper the cultivation of the land e.g. Ibo, *Ala*, and some determine the good conduct of the society, e.g. Mende, *Hum'i*. We have already referred to the rivers of Ghana and to *Tano* in particular. These gods can offer considerable help when invoked, and so man bends his will to their dictates. But there are, however, ultimate situations in which they do not satisfy man's desires. Their devotees may be committed to them but their commitment tends to be incomplete. Drought, famine and the crises of life call for a more effective presence. So God is postulated as the supreme Spirit. He is supreme over all. All the spirits derive their power from Him and in the ultimate crises He is Lord over all.[29] Meanwhile, it is believed that He is not readily accessible to man; at the same time, as if by contradiction, man is always able to call on Him in times of personal distress. Man's sleeping and waking up are also His concern. Every action good or bad is said to be ultimately sanctioned by Him. So, the Mende, for example, always end their prayers to the ancestors or the lesser divinities with the recurrent phrase *ŋgewɔ jahun* i.e. 'by the Sovereign will of God'. God is now the great Presence. He is everywhere and is generally associated with

16

the sky or the firmament – Akan, *Nyame*, the Lunar Mother-goddess or *Nyan-kopon*, the Sun; Yoruba, ɔlɔrun, the owner of Heaven. The Kono of Sierra Leone call Him *yataa*, 'He whom you meet everywhere'. But His presence is not felt directly, except in brief spells, when He is invoked by means of individual ejaculations. Creation, jural authority and Providence are attributed to Him. But the lesser spirits control the everyday life of mankind.

The West African concept of God thus provides a Presence, which seems to be somewhat real but only in times of crises. Operational presence is vested in the ancestral spirits and Nature deities, with which are associated covenantal relations with man. But covenants between man and his gods must be reflected in the relationships between man and man. Of the various covenantal relations, the blood-covenant is perhaps the most exacting. In the present context, it is the most permanent manifestation of presence – usually demonic. To violate a blood-covenant, it is believed, is to be doomed to certain death. Blood is life. When therefore one person eats of the blood of a partner, it is assumed that the blood continues to flow intact in the blood-stream of the eater and will rise up as a hostile life-force, from within, to destroy him if he turns traitor. In effect, then, the blood-covenant represents a relationship because of which, the I having first absorbed the life-blood of the Thou into his system is as a result in symbiosis with the Thou, who is with him at all times, ready to strike whenever he defaults. Conscience now becomes identified with the I of the individual. And yet, alas! man is still goaded on by fears of witches and various spirits. Only when we examine the Religion of the Hebrews and later of the Jews, do we meet earliest instance of God as a Covenantal Presence. To the Hebrew, God as the essence of Being and the foundation of all existence is closely associated with two cardinal factors, viz., Promise and Covenant. The totality of all existence, domestic, commercial and political was therefore embedded in a concept of Covenant. Yaweh transcended all tribal relations as the Prophets taught. So He was grieved when short-balances were used by mercenary Hebrew tradesmen as well as when Tyre delivered up (for destruction) the people of Edom and 'did not remember the covenant of brotherhood' (Amos 8:5, 1:9). His Covenant and Promise were indeed not only with the Patriarchs, Abraham, Isaac and Jacob, but even with those who were alive at the time of the Deuteronomic Writers, 'Even with us, who are all of us alive this day', (Dt 5:2 f cp 29:10), they said. God is now more expressly thought of in terms of specific human analogies, derived from direct experience. So the Jews postulated the *Shekinah*. Transcendence has come close to immanence in the concept of God.

THE DOGMA OF SUPER-SIZE

The Kposso maintain that when the High God Uwolowu wanted to create the diseases He 'took fire and cold. Fire is the disease, cold is the allevation. He then said to a man by the name of Sropa, "If you are cold, don't go to the fire!" But Sropa did go to the fire nevertheless . . . Uwolowu then made Ikono ("a bird with rust-brown feathers") fly out of the fire. This bird beat Sropa with its wings, and leprosy broke out on his body. Since then Ikono's sound reminds man of Sropa's disobedience.'[1] A telling story this, quite typical of other stories in West Africa relating to the origin of sickness and death.

But when we begin to ask ourselves questions about the hidden meaning, we are left puzzled. In ordinary African communities, men, women and children gather round the fire on cold days to warm themselves; at night they sit around a fire and amuse each other, by telling stories, or by singing and dancing. Quite often the fire provides the only cheer at night in an otherwise dark village with no street lamps to relieve the nocturnal gloom. Of course fire burns. It is believed that if one spent too much time close to a fire, one develops a wrinkle of the skin. But the Kposso have attributed leprosy to man's desire to warm himself when he felt cold. As the story stands, out from within the fire there sprang the dreadful bird Ikono which beat Sropa's body with its wings, thus explaining the presence of the scaly impression which the skin develops when it becomes very dry. True, the story is built around the incidence of leprosy, but it is important to note that the moral of the disastrous results of disobedience has also been thrown in. It would be interesting to know whether the Kposso thought of leprosy in terms of the Bible usage or of modern medical terminology.[2] In spite of the improbability of getting an accurate answer to this question, one might say that the Kposso have produced an atypical and unnatural interpretation to a most natural behaviour, by introducing the bird Ikono as the harbinger of disaster, in this case leprosy; the colour of whose 'rust-brown feathers' is attributed to the fact that it came out of the fire which God had created. This introduction of an atypical

18

and unnatural cause to an otherwise unrelated but disastrous effect is what we shall discuss in this article under the title *"The Dogma of Super-Size"*. In Sierra Leone instances of this dogma abound at two levels, human and sub-human. Firstly, we intend to discuss some of these as seen in (i) Super-normality in animals, (ii) Sex and sex-relations.

1. INSTANCES OF SUPER-NORMALITY OF SIZE OR BEHAVIOUR

(i) Among the Mende, an animal of supernormal size, be it goat or cow, is known as *hani-waa*, i.e. a big thing, which is therefore revered as possessing qualities which are unusual and, perhaps the abode of some influence greater than man. It is certainly not true to type. It is interesting to note here that the Konde of Tanganyika who call God *Kyala* or *Lesa*, also call anything great, oxen or even he-goat, *Kyala*, implying thereby that God 'takes up His temporary abode' in them.[3]

(ii) Again twins are revered by all groups, Mende, Temne, Creoles, because they have not been born in the typical form of the usual single sibling. They are thought to be highly psychic and therefore possessing very unusual psychic powers. Indeed, one hears twins saying of themselves, 'I am a twin, you must not trifle with me.' It is believed that they sometimes contract between themselves to kill one or other of their parents. The death of one of them in infancy is sometimes thought to be the result of a struggle between them; at other times it is said that the one who died decided to return to the place whence it came. Various rites are therefore performed around the birth of twins.

In former days, when children were always born at home and only later were they brought into the other parts of the house and into the outside world, small tiny white beads were strung together and tied around their left arms or their left feet; they were then dressed up and laid in a winnowing fan and taken around the neighbourhood. This seemed to have been the sum-total of the Creole rituals. But among the Mende several women formed a procession, all dancing and singing around the twins. Salt, pepper and uncooked rice, and two strips of shirting, in one yard lengths were placed in the fan, the food and condiments symbolising the staff of life and the shirting, the essential clothing required for ordinary life. These women, friends of the mother, would then solicit gifts from the members of the neighbourhood almost anticipatory of the modern provision of public support for quads and quintuplets. Among the Creoles and Mende, when the twins were old enough to eat normal foods, a special diet was prepared – 'twin-food', consisting of beans, generally boiled and mixed with red palm oil, and sometimes also crushed and fried in red palm-oil (among Creoles) and plant-ains, were served to them. Such preparations were repeated at regular intervals and served to the twins, the assumption being that this type of meal tempers their hyper-psychic tendencies. In view of the fact that the two bean-meals and the plantain dish are often found among the meals prepared for votive offerings to the dead, one may infer that twins are thought to be kin to the ancestral spirits. The Sherbro hold similar rituals but in addition build twin houses, small circular mud-huts in which they set a mound of black ant-hill. This ant-hill usually symbolises the dead ancestors, who live underground and are not seen, but are known to be alive and active. It could therefore be said that twins are widely regarded as super-natural and are accorded a deference which the normal sibling never enjoys.

(iii) *Bird-Calls*. We shall mention two categories of these calls.
(a) Bird-calls in the lonely forests. Often a traveller believes that the call of a certain bird augurs success or failure in his enterprise according as the bird calls from along the right or left side of the road in the direction in which he travels. To some of us this sounds so arbitrary a judgment in view of the fact that, taken strictly, if when the bird calls, there happens to be another person travelling in the opposite direction, if he also assumes the same interpretation of the calls, he would be destined to failure whilst his opposite number would be joyfully speeding on to success. Not so! We must not, however, think of life in the deep forests in early times in terms of modern communications and travelling. Many people did not travel singly among the forest paths except on urgent immediate business. In any case each man lived in his own world. We must remember that a lone traveller would be engrossed with his thoughts as he went his way alone. The call of a bird might shake him from his brown study and give him a feeling of companionship. In addition, he would have been brought up on the notion that the right hand represents graciousness, favours and other aspects of propriety. It is that which is used for eating. The left hand represented the opposite. What more then than for the lone African traveller to interpret a bird call along

20

the right side of the forest path as suggestive of a favour of one sort or the other, and in particular as an augury of success. Since the bird is likely to hop from one side of the path to the other, it therefore follows that whenever it does happen that two travellers are walking in opposite directions they may hear its call from both sides of the path and so give identical interpretations to it as symbolising success.

(b) The call of owls and giant bats (vampire bats). The hoot of the owl is universally believed to be an indication that witches are abroad and planning the destruction of some innocent but predetermined victim. Since it is believed that witches can invest themselves in an owl, this interpretation of the owl's call is readily understandable.[4]

The drawling call of the giant bat is also believed to represent the activity of witches. The caw-caw-caw-crrrrrrr of this bat is said to indicate the resultant sucking noise when a child's blood is being drained off its body by the witch investing the bird. So deeply ingrained is the fear of this bat that the writer knows the case of a man who was firmly convinced that he suffered from hemiphlegia because he had shot at one of these bats.

Behind these two cases of bird-calls lies the element of super-normality. Members of the bird-world go to sleep at dusk except for the night-jar, the bat and the owl, who sleep all day and prowl about at night. The unusualness of the physical build of the bat lends further weight to the primary feeling of awesomeness associated with its feeding habits.

(iv) *Strange-looking animals and insects*
(a) *The chameleon*. This animal has the special physical endowment, as everyone knows, of adapting its colouration to that of its environment, thus producing a perfect camouflage in self-defence. Such an animal naturally becomes elusive because in terms of *gestalt* it is difficult to track its movements. Indeed, it can perfectly elude anyone who wishes to attack it. But it also possesses other puzzling characteristics. Normally it walks slowly, taking long strides as it goes along. But it also demonstrates an unexpected speed of locomotion when it is in danger of being attacked. Its sudden leap and rapid movements are so unexpected that an onlooker is left standing aghast. It also has two large eyes bulging unusually far out of its head, which stand on swivels and are capable of looking towards two different directions at the same time. This is more than mere unusualness to the primitive man. Lastly, a fat, well-fed looking chameleon is hard to find. This animal is always skinny, with protruding ribs jutting out of its sides, a pot-belly appearance and somewhat seemingly sunken temples.

It is therefore regarded as of supernormal qualities. Among the Yoruba, for example, it is the animal which Olodumare is said to have sent to inspect the solid earth when it was first formed.[5] In Sierra Leone, it is thought to be against the well-being of an unborn child if the pregnant mother encounters one. In particular, it is thought that the chameleon can exercise an evil influence upon children and they then contract what is known among the Creoles as 'chameleon disease'. This is a wasting disease, the symptoms of which are flaccidity of the muscles due to dehydration, protruding ribs, a pot-belly, sunken temples, prominent eyeballs (proptoma), long tapering extremities, general lassitude and a general loss of body tone. Many children die of it. The general appearance of the patient seems to suggest that of a chameleon. Medically, the disease is caused by chronic avitaminosis. The Creoles, however, attribute it to the chameleon and so perform specially devised rites to relax its grip on the patients.

(b) *Auspicious Insects. The Stick Insect.* This is an insect with long sprawling legs and no wings, which often crawls into huts and sometimes dwelling houses and rests, fixed, on the walls. It sometimes assumes a rampant attitude with all its legs widely spread out. At other times it assumes a recumbent posture, and stands on the walls with its legs folded up together, looking like a thin twig jutting out horizontally from the wall. It may be that the insect is out on an innocent hunting expedition, waiting patiently for some careless victim to come its way. But among the Creoles, for instance, its presence betokens a death, that of a close relative if recumbent, or of a distant relation is in a rampant posture. Here again, unusualness is the answer to the attitude held towards this insect. The praying mantis, its nearest relation, has wings, is green and is known to be a vicious hunter of flies or cockroaches or of its male lover. The stick insect is usually brown, similar to the colour of brown soil, such as was often used to build huts. Because of its natural colouration, it is not, however, easy to detect its presence. Nor do I think that the ordinary person has ever stopped to ask whether it is usually waiting for a prey or not. But it is strange-looking by all standards. So it is looked upon with an attitude of eeriness, which is all the more emphasized by the fact that it is known to assume the two postures referred to earlier.

(c) *The Bumble Bee.* This is a beetle which generally flies into a house buzzing as it enters, then falls on its back, continuing its buzz. Most Sierra Leoneans, Creole, Mende and Temne, interpret the appearance of this beetle as an augury of a visitor, and a welcome one too. In a country which abounds in beetles and other kindred insects, it is interesting to note that this beetle whilst displaying the musical buzz-buzz of most members of the beetle family, generally drops in front of one of the inmates of the house into which it comes, rolls on its back for a few minutes and then flies off. Unlike other beetles, it is clean and is not a pest at all. In appearance it has quite a pleasant colouration – sometimes bright green with a U-shaped yellow band running along the edge of the upper part of its body. So, in contrast to, say, the dung-beetle, with its unattractive colouration and its revolting habit of rolling dung around in a spherical ball, the bumble bee is unusually pleasant and welcome in its own right. So its presence is regarded as betokening a welcome arrival.

(v) *Signs of genius or extraordinary ability in men*
Among the Kono, it is believed that possession of super-normal ability – persuasive oratory, a telling personality, superior success in business, is due to the possession of a 'witch's cloak' (*witch-gown*).[6] It is said to be generally in the form of a cloak, but other forms of garment or a hammock or a piece of cloth, the size of a handkerchief, are talked of. The owner of a cloak is said to be endowed with extraordinary powers. It is said to be invisible to the uninitiated eye and that only initiates can perceive it. It is also claimed that there are grades of these cloaks or the other forms which have been mentioned and that the costlier the cloak the more powerful it is. Each is said to be fitted with 'witch' armaments, the whole outfit being strung directly on to the owner's heart. As a result not only is excellent performance attributed to the witch's cloak, but various other corollary factors are attributed to it. For example, a sudden squall towards the end of a humid tropical day with sharp lightning flashes followed by successive, reverberating peals of thunder are attributed to a war among owners of the cloak. It is believed that owners of cloaks of inferior quality must defer to those who hold more costly ones. Otherwise, the stronger armed man would fall on the weaker and seize his cloak. The lightning and thunder which to us naturally follow the heat in a season when there is much humidity in the atmosphere is usually attributed to the struggle between the contenders. Again, because it is believed that the garment is strung on to the heart of its owner, it is also believed that during a struggle as mentioned above, the powerfully armed cloak-owner captures that of his victim, snatches the garment, and therefore in taking it away, tears off its strings from the heart of its owner. Naturally the victim falls down and dies, blood gushing out of his mouth as he does so. To us this would be death as a result of a haemorrhage caused by the rupture of a blood vessel – it may be in the stomach, as in the

case of a stomach ulcer, peptic or duodenal, or perhaps in the lungs as in the case of pulmonary tuberculosis. But to the Kono, anyone who dies of a haemorrhage bringing up some fresh blood as a result is invariably said to have possessed a witch-gown which had been snatched from him by the possessor of a more powerful one.

Here again supernormality is the basis of the arguments. The man of genius, the powerful orator, the man of impressive personality, the successful business man and men of similar qualities are unusual. So they must possess an additional source of power or influence. Death by internal bleeding is strange to those who only understand death by sickness or from exterior bleeding. So the effusion of warm blood just when a person is about to die must be the result of a rupture of the heart. What to us is the rupture of a blood vessel, usually arterial, is explained as the rupture of the heart itself.

We may recall here the suggestion by Mircea Eliade that perfection in any sphere is frightening and that it is regarded as sacred or a magic quality, which even in civilised societies is felt when men come face to face with a genius or a saint.[7]

2. INSTANCES OF SUPER-NORMALITY OF THE HUMAN FEMALE – SEX AND SEXUAL RELATIONS

This is a man's world, and the criteria of human existence are based on the male. The woman therefore with her special physical make-up is therefore unusual. Even in the most civilised societies the uncanny intuition of 'woman' is regarded as a quality not usually found in the male. In less developed communities, prominence is given to the fact that woman bears children only when impregnated by a male. She is known to be sought after by males as the medium through which the male can satisfy the most intense of his bodily desires, the sex urge. Add to this, the monthly experience of losing menstrual blood makes her strikingly different from the male. Primitive man understood the consequential henosis of the sex-act as well as the need for sleep after it and so imposed various tabus to ensure this.[8] He also regarded 'woman' with some dread. In this article we shall limit ourselves to only a few of the implications associated with the sex-organism of the woman and with the sex-act.

(a) Among the Creoles, it is generally believed that the performance of the sex-act during the day, especially in the morning hours, will cause a man to fail in any enterprise he embarks upon. This is a way of saying that after a daylight affair, when a man is never usually able to go off to sleep and recover the energy that he loses during the climax of the sex-act he is never settled enough to conduct the day's business adequately, the more so in cases which demand physical energy.

(b) The Temne maintain that the performance of the sex-act has a definite influence upon crops which are planted on the following day. So 'a farmer must practice continence during the planting or reaping season'. He must not touch his wife on the 'night before a farm is cleared of bush, or hoed'. If a man 'cohabits with his wife on the eve of cassava planting' it is believed that the crop 'will be bitter'.[9] So also when boys are circumcised, 'the woman who cooks' for the patients 'must not have connection either the night before or during the time she is cooking, or the wounds will be long in healing'.[10] Even the father of a boy who has been circumcised may not wash his sores 'for if he had cohabited the night before, the sores would grow larger.'[11] The woman, because she apparently plays a passive role in procreation, is believed to have an adverse influence upon the crops she plants. If she plants 'groundnuts or koko yams' after union with her husband, 'all the husks or tubers will be empty.' The Temne also believe that if a man goes on a business journey and meets with failure, his wife must have committed adultery in his absence. So, too, it is believed that if a man who has had relations with women 'climbs a kola-tree' all the pods will be empty.[12] Of course, a menstruant woman may not plant anything. Similar notions exist in other tribes along West Africa. Among the Kwotto of Northern Nigeria a woman is not allowed to touch the weapons of a hunter and among several Ibo tribes strict continence is observed during the planting season.[13] Among the Ashanti a woman should not touch a drum nor carry it. The Ntumpane drums of the Akan are 'taboo to menstruating women'.[14] Woman is regarded as one of the two worst destructive forces when she has her menses, death being the next. Water or cloth which has been in contact with the pudenda is believed by the Akan as being capable of destroying supernatural influences as well as maliciously procuring evil.[15] It seems that the determinant in all these attitudes to 'women' is the unusualness of the female sex – the physical make up of the female sex organs and their role during the sex-act, and the effect of sex-union on the male.[16] The detumescence of the male organ that follows the sex-act naturally leaves the husband inert, in contrast to his usual physical vigour. The dissemination of seed leaves him seminally empty and therefore unproductive for a period – perhaps long or short according as the physical processes are understood. So crops planted soon after are by an assumed process of empathy non-productive. A fortiori, the woman

25

who it could be assumed has this deleterious influence on the male can more readily transfer the same influence to any crops she plants and even more so, to the male sex-organ with a wound on it after circumcision (cp. Gen. xxxiv. 24 ff). She must naturally possess super-normal powers to be able to knock a man flat after the sex act.

Again, in view of the fact that bleeding naturally leads to a man's death, a woman is all the more unusual during her years of sex-vitality, when she regularly loses much blood every month and never dies. The menstruant woman therefore symbolises an object of supernormal powers; in particular, she is regarded as possessing such powers as are resistant to death. What is easier, then, than to infer further that she is inherently as destructive as death? So the pudenda of a menstruant woman are thought to be death-radiating and at a childbirth more actively so. Among the Mende it used to be believed that if a man was present at a childbirth he would die.

We could multiply instances to illustrate the predominance of this attitude to nature and life if space permitted. What, then, is the significance of this aspect of the Dogma of Super-Size? We would say that it is indicative of the attitude of 'primitive' man, Mircea Eliade would say 'traditional' man, towards Nature and Life. He saw the unusual features of life, manifestations of the sacred – an 'exterior force that differentiates it from its milieu and give it meaning and life.'[17] He naturally believes in a Supreme Being, but this belief undergoes stages of valuation and revaluation all the more so because the Supreme Being is not readily demonstrable. In particular, primitive man suffers from the discomfort which nature imposes upon him. Why does a woman bear twins instead of siblings and so give the impression that she belongs to the world of the lower animals most of whom produce a litter at paturition? Add to this the physical discomfort of the successive birth-pangs, and the social and economic problems that come of rearing them. Or again, why does an owl, unlike most other birds, not only feed on rats and other small animals, but also fly about at night when most other living animals are asleep? Similar questions may be posed when the bat is considered. The Mendes talk of a bat as *Gbavɛ ñoi-ma*, which I would interpret to mean 'by way of difference from a bird', and so 'a bird with a difference', neither beast nor bird; the bat has a mouselike face. The chameleon and the stick insect manifest distinctive qualities which also make them suggestive of human discomfort; in the one case, the child weakened by a wasting disease with its ribs protruding out of its sides and in the other the motionless corpse of a near or

26

distant relation. Behind all this there lies the great question 'Does the experience of evil – especially suffering and death – come from the Supreme Being, and, if so, are these objects which suggest the presence of various forms of Evil, symbols of the presence of the Supreme Being?' And here we might recall Jung's definition of a Symbol as 'the best possible description, or formula, of a relatively unknown fact; a fact, however, which is none the less recognized or postulated as existing'.[18] It is in this context that distinctions as 'knowable' and 'unknowable' become relevant. Modern scientific thinking will not countenance the Dogma of Super-Size because it is not demonstrable. But in real fact the real values of life, love, beauty and truth represent the absolutely unknowable. Modern man may find this attitude to life irrational. On the other hand, reason is not everything. The aspect of the Dogma of Super-Size we have been discussing may seem to be based on unreason. But it has been a reservoir of psychological comfort to those who lived in the tropical forest world of the African Continent.

3. THE OMNIPOTENCE OF THOUGHT

In the previous section we examined some instances of the application of the Dogma of Super-Size to external objects. As we saw then, certain objects, some human, were thought of as possessing powers or indicating supernatural abilities because of their natural physical constitution. But 'Primitive man believes also in the efficacy of gestures, objects and words to bring some desired goal within his reach, if they in some manner reflect his desire to give it visible shape'.[19] That is to say, he believes in the subjective possession of power by human beings as a constituent of their make-up. Such power it is assumed resides in human thought. It may be set in motion explicitly by the use of words accompanied by the appropriate gestures or implicitly in unuttered speech – the silent speech of the Behaviourist School of Psychology. Thus in the 1930's there raged in Nigeria, what was then known as the *Yola*-formula, 'It is nothing at all, koko-yam!', which was 'accredited with power to make chains drop from a prisoner and enable him to escape; to cause bullets just breeze past a soldier in the battle front, so that he escapes unscathed; to make spears and arrows fall harmlessly at his side, and to cause knife stabs to have no effect.'[20] In particular, there was a man, Alabi by name, who came to be known as 'the wonder man of Abeokuta.' It was alleged that when Alabi was imprisoned in the Native

Administration prison he was able to escape by using this formula. As it happened, he came under the notice of the police who placed him under lock and key in a guarded cell and he did not escape. In the language of the author of *Renascent Africa*, 'He was hand-cuffed and securely locked up in H.M. Prisons and there he remained.'[21] More often one meets with cases of 'induction' of power through the spoken word. Two instances will illustrate the type: In Sierra Leone, for example to keep thieves from spoiling farms, certain protective charms are set in the farms, some of them noticeable, others not. If a thief does take away any of the crops, he will be expected to fall ill, say, from some severe form of dysentery or vomiting or both. He has to confess his theft in time or else he is expected to continue to get increasingly worse and ultimately die. Confession of the crime however makes it possible for certain propitiatory offerings to be made and a herbal cure prepared; in a few days, the patient recovers. The protective charm itself is often singularly disappointing; the stub of a firewood, a skeleton of a land tortoise; a piece of calabash to which may be attached the vine of a creeper (Mende – *hɔɔɛi* – *Costus afer*) usually used to indicate a taboo, a soap-stone carving or some other object of little or no apparent significance. But the significant factor is the rite of consecrating the firewood, or the skeleton of the tortoise or the soap-stone or what have you. In the particular case, of the firewood, all one does is to choose a short stub of a used piece of firewood; one ties it to a pole of any length one chooses, erects it in the farm and then 'talks' to it, that is to say, commissions it to guard and punish any trespassers with violent stomach pains or some equally unpleasant ailment. At the same time, care is always taken to provide for the man who is desperately hungry and comes upon a farm with, say, root crops which may satisfy him if he was hungry. Should such a person root up a cassada plant, for example, he was more likely to eat it on the spot. The truly hungry man, often hungry because he is on a long journey and is therefore far away from home, is of course not interested in taking any extra food away from the farm thereby adding to the impedimenta which he is carrying. So whilst the stub of firewood is being commissioned to take stern measures against thieves, it is at the same time given a venial clause: 'May no harm come to those who because of sheer hunger come to this farm and root up any food crops e.g. a cassada plant, and eat the same in the farm.' Similarly among the Temnes of Sierra Leone, if a woman comes upon a peculiarly shaped stone in the bed of a stream, or a pebble with a colour different from the rest in a given pile, she would take it home, keep it in a receptacle together with a few cowries, and then place some rich flour in the

28

receptacle using some special words at the same time. Henceforth she regards the stone as possessing supernatural powers and capable of providing her with such things as she desires. It is no longer a mere stone or pebble; it is now endowed with the capacity to understand the demands of its owner and to satisfy them as well. We are of the opinion that the same notions account for the *Shigidi* in Nigeria. This is primarily a clay model of a man, about one foot in height, into which special powers are said to be induced by the appropriate incantations said by a *babalawo*. When the rites have been completed, it is claimed that the image becomes capable of locomotion and can be sent to a great distance on a mission to inflict harm on a person, usually to kill him.

When we were boys, we believed that we could stave off punishment for misbehaviour, by casting a spell over, 'tying' as we termed it, the offended adults – teachers or more so adult relations. The tying process consisted of making small knots on the frond of an oil-palm branch, and expressing the wish that 'so and so' may not recall the offence. Interesting enough, we were successful most of the time, or we seemed to be. Sometimes no words were uttered; our intentions were left unsaid although prominent in our thoughts. But in every case, the knotted palm frond was given a significance outside its intrinsic value.

An explicit instance of the power associated with the unuttered speech is found in the use in Sierra Leone of the saliva in one's mouth, used as a curative for a stiff neck, provided it is applied to the neck before the sufferer speaks to any member of the household. It may be that the act of massaging the neck, made easy by concentrated saliva formed in the mouth during sleep, is the real cure. But to our people, the cure is attributed to the saliva used. Similarly a curse uttered without first speaking to anyone is thought to be of greater potency than otherwise. It seems that the various *orishas* of the Yoruba, – *Shango*, the thunder cult, *Shopponu* the small-pox cult and *Ogun*, the cult of hunters and blacksmiths prominently so – are of like origin. Our interpretation of the Yoruba situation is confirmed by Ulli Beier's suggestion that the word for prayer in Yoruba, '*she orisha*' means 'make the god'.[22] We would go on to say that the various totems which abound are created in the same way as the *orishas* of the Yoruba. Among the Akan for example a totem is thought to be the incarnation of the *obosom*, the deity which a clan worships. Eva Meyerowitz tells us that 'in the dim past' a woman was occasionally 'possessed by the life-giving spirit of the moon Mother-goddess, and in that ecstatic state gave life to an *obosom*', who was 'personified as a goddess and given a name, so

29

that people might address her in prayer'. The woman who thus brought an *obosom* to being became the Elder woman of a group of people who gathered around her. When circumstances such as a food shortage, or scarcity of water or an impending attack of an enemy required the people to move their original home, 'an antelope, a wild falcon, a leopard or some other animal would guide them to more fertile earth or to water, or would lead them to safety by taking them to a ford across a river, or to a cave where they could hide.' 'This animal was . . . thereupon venerated as divine' and regarded as the incarnation of the *obosom*.[23] Similar notions exist among other tribes who do not introduce any 'incarnation' theory. The totemic animal is sometimes identified with the founder of a clan or tribe or it may be just an ordinary animal which by some peculiar chance happened to save the clan from serious misadventure of one sort or another. Thus the *Kwotto* of Northern Nigeria say that a lion was seen standing over the grave of the first chief of the lion clan and henceforth it was believed to be the embodiment of the spirit of that chief. So they refer to a lion as 'grandfather'. Again, we are told that on the night when a hostile band of superior forces from one village were going to sack a neighbouring village, a crocodile appeared at the point where they had to cross a stream and, prevented them from destroying the village. The chief of the village which was to have been attacked and destroyed, first declared the crocodile their friend and saviour, and later raised it to the status of the village totem. Almost all totems seem to be traceable to similar origins. The tribe or clan believe that an animal or (sometimes but not often) a tree has been influential in their escape from danger. They owe their existence to it and go on to interpret the life-saving event as the manifestation, on the physical plane, of events which first took place in the distant unknown on a spiritual plane.

J.T. Alldridge, gives an interesting account of indirect induction in his description of the *minsereh* images used for divination by members of the *Yassi* Society in the Sherbro District of Sierra Leone. First of all the *Yassi* Society prepares a 'medicine' which is a concoction of various kinds of vegetable and animal matter, and which after preparation is given a sacredness which must not be violated. Then the *Minsereh* images have power induced into them by being anointed with the *Yassi* medicine. After having been anointed, they are placed by the side of the medicine in order that they may be able to communicate with it. A *Minsereh* image so anointed is then believed to be able to make the official, next in order to the head of the cult, known as *Yamama* to fall asleep and dream. Upon her waking up, the image is re-anointed before being removed

30

from the presence of the 'medicine'; the *Yamama* is not allowed to speak to the image until the re-anointing takes place. But afterwards, she could 'invoke its fetish influence to prevent whatever was impending for good or evil'.[24] Sometimes one finds a case of pure thought at work. Sidney de La Rue tells of the *Boh* cult in the Boozie country in Liberia where the elders are reputed to be capable of 'thinking' a criminal 'dead' and, if he is a tribesman, he dies.[25]

To those who have received Western education and have learnt to associate 'cause and effect' with the known physical laws, the instances which have been listed above make little sense. But for those who accept primitive ways of thinking, two factors deserve consideration: First, to the primitive African, a word means the proper use of the thing for which it stands,[26] and so he assumes that by performing certain 'rites of consecration' an ordinary object, a stone or a tree, ceases to be a mere something and acquires 'a new dimension of sacredness.'[27] Accordingly a hierophany or a kratophany is postulated. Secondly, primitive Africans find that life is full of discomfort and so substitute for the world as they know it another that is humanly motivated and directed. This attitude affords a pleasure which they cannot enjoy in the world when considered in mechanistic terms. In other words, primitive man recasts the universe into human terms.[28] This attitude is of course not a primitive substitute for science. The difference between modern science and mythical thought 'lies not in the quality of the intellectual process but in the nature of the things to which it is applied. Steel axe is better than a stone axe not because one is better made but because steel is a different thing from stone.'[29]

Let us now try to make an assessment of the instances described above. First the case of the '*Yola formula*', and similar claims like the ability to think a man dead. Dr. Azikwe comments adversely against all such claims. 'Do you believe' he asks, 'that an African can poison his fellow-man without seeing him? If so why were the Sedition Bill[30] and other unpopular Bills allowed to remain in the statute book? Probably Europeans are immune from African medicine! If so why are Africans not immune from European bullets?'[31] He then goes on to say, 'Because the primitive educational system of the African is not empirical, he trains his mind to believe in a sort of super-scientific structure which may transcend the theory of relativity. If it is possible to reduce this African Super Science to a scientific basis a fifth dimension is possible'.[32] Dr. Azikwe contends that if the ideas behind these claims are real they should be demonstrable. We would differ from this writer and say that the ideas expressed are in fact not demonstrable because they are the product

31

of certain premises which depend for their validity on the psychological reactions of those who hold them. This is true particularly so of the cases of induction to which reference was made earlier. It must be remembered that in primitive society, a whole series of educational activities goes on by which the mind of the young is conditioned to accept certain forms of behaviour as the bases of their life. In particular, they accept the notion as mentioned above that the word (uttered or unuttered) corresponds to the essence of the thing for which it is used. We would express the view that there therefore develops in any primitive community a *communis sensus* which guides their way of life. Thus the *Mende* of Sierra Leone do always seem to be able to tell, often by oracular divination, it must be granted, whether a protective charm on a farm or the *Humɔi* taboos have been violated. The Akan also use divination methods to discover whether the *ntorɔ* rules have been violated. In short, one may say that there is a catalogue of unwritten diagnoses with the appropriate recipes preserved in an unwritten pharmacopaeia. The cure always includes confession, sacrifices and absolution followed by ritual washing, all of them being components of a propitiatory rite. Again, the illness seems to be fundamentally associated with a psychological condition. Two men may root up plants from the same farm; one eats the tubers on the spot because he is hungry, the other collects a quantity to take home; the later falls ill subsequently whilst the former suffers no ill consequence. Is this due to auto-suggestion based on the accepted forms of the *communis sensus* of the environment? Where this *communis sensus* is no longer accepted no ill effects seem to follow a violation of the taboos. Thus for example young boys who attend school and therefore have begun to question the effectiveness of such taboos, urinate on the medicine placed, say, on a pile of wood to prevent its being stolen. They behave according to a preconceived pattern. A group of boys enters the farm; one of them urinates on the medicine and the others carry the wood out of the farm for even distribution later on. But, perhaps because they still unconsciously accept the validity of the taboo, we are reliably informed that the boy who urinates on the medicine later develops pains in the groin. We have also been told of another method used to avoid the curse of the taboo by school boys. In this case, the medicine is bodily removed from the pile of wood by a member of a group and then the rest carry the wood out, to be evenly shared, later on. These boys work on the principle that the medicine always assumes that only its master – the one who set it up – would move it from the pile of wood. So once it has been moved out to a distant place it no longer feels responsible to guard the wood. In any case

32

confirmed thieves never take any notice of a 'medicine' set over any property and they seem never to be hurt by it.

Again, among the Mende of Sierra Leone, men are forbidden to spy on the proceedings of the *Sande* (*Bondo*) Society which is exclusive to women, or on women masked as *Bondo* devils when they go to some secluded place to remove the carved hollow wooden head-gears for some airing. It is alleged that a man who spies on the women will suffer from elephantiasis of the scrotum. In this context a hydrocele is thought to be an incipient stage of this elephantiasis. Of course, suspicious perhaps of a closed women's society, the men naturally resort to spying on their proceedings in the sacred bush and on their movements during a public performance. Their only opportunity is to spy on the women either as they perform the initiation rites in the sacred bush or when masked.[33] The association of scrotal elephantiasis with a *Sande* taboo is striking when considered in the light of other forms of cultic protection for women. It is said that if the women ever caught a man spying on them in the bush, they handle him roughly, tugging wildly at his genitals and so disabling him. Several of their victims are said to have developed a hydrocelic condition probably caused by the rupture of the blood vessels of the scrotum. Accordingly, cases of elephantiasis of the scrotum and of hydroceles were associated with *Sande* taboo because the filaria worm was not known. Significantly enough, this disease used to be quite prevalent up to say twenty-five years ago especially in the Bonthe and Pujehun districts of the South-Western Province. It should be noted that the so-thought peeping-Toms take good care never to be discovered because public opinion would be greatly against them; and yet up to the present time, i.e. 1963, Mende men who suffer from that condition are thought to have received their just deserts for transgressing the code of the *Sande* Society. We know of no propitiatory rites designed to offer a cure. Such cures as have been obtained are the result of surgical treatment only. Against the popular theory we have mentioned, Lieutenant John Matthews R.N. writing from Sierra Leone in 1785 and 1787, says, in one of his letters, that 'The disease they (i.e. the natives of Sierra Leone) are most subject to are intermitting fevers and the hydrocele; the latter is supposed to be caused by the too frequent use of palm wine, and excess of venery.'[34] Again, if Sidney de la Rue is correct, the criminal, who is 'thought dead and dies in Boozie country, need not know that he had been 'thought' dead. Of course it is possible that the so-called 'thought-projection' is a formalization of an earlier administration of a slow poison which in fact takes effect at the precise time – when the 'thinking dead' ritual is in progress. I do not

33

know that the adults whom we offended ever did appreciate our efforts to hypnotize them not to remember our misbehaviour. Whilst it would be easy to dismiss the childish practices in which we as boys indulged to keep ourselves free from punishment, it is not easy to ignore the claims for thought-protection which have been made by men of some literary and scientific standing.[35] If this theory of thought-protection is admitted, then the boyish pranks in which some of us indulged would readily come under that category. Jahnheinz Jahn would say that these phenomena are possible because 'the African has more faith in the power of the word (uttered or unuttered) than in the power of the substance . . .'[36] We therefore have two types of thought-processes implied in the various instances already discussed: First, cases of violations of taboos which lead to sickness; the offenders are usually not seen in the act, but they fall ill and only recover after a ritual confession, absolution and washing. This seems to be caused by anxiety generated by auto-suggestion induced by an acceptance of the mores of the community and self-condemnation. Secondly, we have cases like the *Boh Cult* or *Shigidi* as interpreted by some[37] in which the individual is alleged to be influenced by the thoughts of others. In both cases the environment plays a great part in the effectiveness either of the taboo or of the course. The case of the *Yola formula* and like instances seem to be based on auto-suggestion.

We would therefore suggest a formula viz, the Power of the Word seated in the soul of the speaker i.e. the Omnipotence of Thought. A strong soul utters a strong word and a weak soul a weak word. But the concept of soul is not limited to man alone in primitive minds. Animals have souls and the trees and stones also have souls. In the language of Pedersen, 'It is a swarm of living souls who fill the earth';[38] man, animals, trees, stones etc., These soul-substances however, as Pedersen tells us, 'cannot exist without volition' and do need motivating influence(s), 'the strength emanating from it and in its turn, reacting upon it.'[39] Pedersen was of course describing the primitive attitude to life. Jahnheinz Jahn makes an almost identical statement with regard to African attitudes. He notes that the Bantu of Ruanda classify substantives into four categories:—

     I Muntu='human being' (plural Bantu)
    II Kintu='thing' (plural Bintu)
   III Hantu='place and time'
   IV Kuntu='modality'

adding that 'everything there is must necessarily belong to one of these four categories and must be conceived of not as substance but

34

as force!' – so 'man is a force, all things are forces, places and time are forces and the 'modalities' are forces.'[40] He then goes to propose that there exists a 'cosmic universal force "NTU" in which Being and beings coalesce' i.e. NTU expresses the being of the forces already referred to. This cosmic universal force however depends on the 'driving power' of what the Bantu calls *Nommo* i.e. the word; it is this *Nommo* which 'gives life and efficacy to all things.' But *Nommo* does not possess any initiative; it depends on *Muntu* which in fact represents both human beings and what we shall call human archetypes; that is to say it includes human beings, living and dead, the *orishas, loas* and *Bon Dieu*. In particular, 'the *Bintu*' (Plural of *Kintu*) 'i.e. plants, animals, minerals, tools, objects of customary usage' are '"frozen" forces, which await the command of a *Muntu*'.[41] Jahn unlike Pedersen includes God as one of the species of *Muntu*, thus predicating of Him the impersonal influence of NTU and restricting Him by the creative power of *Nommo*. In other words, the primitive African like the Hebrews thinks of life in terms of a 'totality' made up of souls of human beings, of animals and of the inanimate world. Thus man can draw power from other substances by approaching them and can also strengthen them by a like approach. In particular huge outcrops of rock like the *Olumo* Rock at Abeokuta and the Great Rock of *Taa Kora* near *Tanoboase* in Ashanti, are classical examples of stones being 'strengthened' by man's approach, themselves in their unusual size, manifesting a hierophany. This strengthening perhaps explains why Africans would not pass on a simple herbal curative without asking for a token fee, sometimes only a penny, but in every case an indication that one is prepared to 'redeem' the curative from its previous owner. It also explains why if one is going to pluck a leaf for medicinal use at night, one is always taught to first shake the leaf and address it. In Freetown, we were taught to say '*Wek, wek a kam pick you,*' i.e. wake up, I have come to pluck you! Only when such a formula has first been repeated, would the herbal cure be expected to be effective.

It is in this context that we must try to understand the reality of the ancestral dead to the African. One often hears that the ancestors appear to their descendants in dreams and often give advice or sharp warning. There have been cases of curative herbs being mentioned in a dream and when used, were found effective. Douglas Warner tells of a young man whose parents had both died and he had no one to 'pay for his schooling.' He had a tearful night but when he fell asleep he dreamt, 'and in his dream his mother appeared before him and gave into his hand three one-pound notes, the cost of the rest of his schooling. He awoke at dawn, the dream vivid in his brain, only to weep again with disappointment when he found no money lying beside his pillow. The next night he did not dream – but in the morning when he woke up he found three pounds lying there. And he took the money, and went to school, and completed his education. When his schooling was ended he went in search of work, and found it. Because he was clever and hardworking he prospered. Each month he managed to put aside a little money saved from his earnings, and dreamed of establishing his own business one day. Then one month's end, he took out of its hiding place the tin box in which he kept his savings, and counted them, and they were three pounds short of the correct total. Puzzled and tearful, he went to bed. That night he dreamed once more, and in his dream his mother came to him and smiled, and said: "Son, go ahead and prosper and do good. The money I lent you has been repaid"'.[42] This fantastic story is an index of what incredible influence is attributed to the ancestral spirits and still more so what claims the dreamers make for their nocturnal subconscious emanations. The Swedish Lutheran Bishop, Dr. Bengt Sundkler, formerly Director of the Swedish Institute of Missionary Research Uppsala, mentions a similar story in his comprehensive study of the Christian Ministry in Africa. Discussing the role of the African Minister in his congregation, he refers to a story related by F. Grebert, a French Missionary in French Equatorial Africa, in his book *Au Gabon* which tells of how some months after the death of a certain catechist his congregation went through a spiritual experience. The story goes: 'Living near an alcoholic factory, the people had eventually become alcoholics and no longer showed any interest in the life of the Church. Suddenly however, they stopped drinking and began as a group to take a lively part in the Church services. One man in the village had in a dream heard the very voice of the deceased catechist calling out, "Return to God"'. The catechist's call in the dream is of course similar to other rebukes attributed to the ancestors; in this case, as it could be in true ancestor worship, the whole village is affected. The catechist's call is a rebuke against their falling away from the Church. Dr. Sundkler's interpretation is interesting though unsatisfactory. He says 'On this level of psychic collective experience are formed strong ties of fellowship between pastor and followers in the Church in Africa.'[43] We need not condemn the attitude if it could be rightly employed in Christian thinking; but it is rather perilous. The dreams we have reported in this study fit into a system. One subconsciously refers back to the old pattern of 'approbations' and 'disapprobations' based on one's early upbringing; and who but one's

36

parents or foster-parents would be most closely identified with the *communis sensus* thus invoked? One could therefore say that the raw material of the symbolism which appears in the dreams is the attitude of those involved, towards their parents and therefore towards the ancestors. They are physically dead but, in fact, now live as spirit and therefore not limited by the circumstances of space and time; as the older members of the family or clan, they are naturally thought to be wiser and more competent to give appropriate advice in times of difficulty. They can also rebuke their descendants for bad behaviour and such rebuke must be heeded or else personal or national disasters may result from the obstinacy which ignores their warnings.

Again, those ancestors who had showed prowess or other forms of excellence during their life-time would after their death be regarded as even more powerful and more proficient in the performance of their skills. So the founding fathers of the clans are thought to be able to continue to exert supreme influence on their descendants and are not regarded as ordinary dead, 'but as those who share in the power of the Supreme Being'.[44] All are better able to do what they practised when alive and in particular to protect, defend and provide for their children. So for example, among the Kwotto, the spirits of the deceased chiefs, the ancestral kings, are called upon to 'give the living rain', whilst those of commoners are invoked to help with the yield of the crops and to 'give fertility to women'.[45] A similar situation exists in Central Polynesia where the spirits of those who die a natural death are supposed to be 'weak and feeble', but those of warriors are 'strong and vigorous'; the enfeeblement caused by sickness being the criterion.[46] As already stated, those spirits may of course become male-volent when angry because of neglect or because of the misbehaviour of one or other descendants and then, they express their displeasure through attendant misfortune. But they need not be so. However, whenever they are, they may be propitiated, and like all good parents, they are always ready to forgive and be of service again.[47] The whole process seems to be essentially psychological.

We must here raise the question of the significance of the sacrifices offered to the totemic spirits and the ancestors.[48] Rattray tells us that 'when the Ashanti before partaking of wine or spirits, pours a little on the ground from the cup, he does so not to the Earth Goddess but for the shades of his ancestors'. Dr. K.A. Busia also points out that at meal times 'the old Ashanti offers the first morsel to the ancestors.' Indeed, it is believed that 'the tribe as a whole is protected by the spirits of the dead rulers.' Accordingly an Ashanti chief is expected to offer libations to his royal ancestors every twenty-one days, on behalf of his subjects, praying that the soil may be fruitful and the land increase. We must recall that when a sacrifice is offered, the offerer first of all identifies himself with the victim or gift offered often by laying his hands on it, thereby declaring that the victim is his representative. This identification indicates that offerer and victim have become devoted to the honour of the god or spirit to which the offering is made. We must also mention that confession, individual or communal, is a vital element in the typical sacrificial rites. Finally, we must note that in the rites involving sacrificial meals, the food is generally shared by several people even when there is only one offerer; this common participation of the sacrificial meal seems to be thought of in terms of the god or spirit sharing in the meal associated with the sacrifice, or the god or totemic spirit itself becoming the food on which the devotees feed. In every case however the sacrificial act constitutes a bond collectively between members of the clan or cult and the god or totem, and severally between the participants – each with the other.[49]

As we have tried to show already, the god or ancestor who is worshipped is in effect the product of the mind and 'strengthened' to the form in which it deserves veneration, because of the effect of the power of human thought. H.J. Rose in a discussion of *Numen* and *Mana* mentions that the purpose of sacrifice is to 'increase' in power, the god to whom the offering is made, 'presumably by receiving the life of the victim, certainly by being fed on such holy food as its duly consecrated flesh, or the cereal offerings, also duly consecrated, which may replace or accompany it.'[50] Elsewhere he and a joint author say that 'to increase the power of a deity by appropriate ritual seems to be the aim and object of ancient sacrifice in its earliest forms before it was thought of as a present to win his favour; . . .'[51] When one examines the ritual employed at the communal sacrifices, one notices that there is generally a meal in which everybody present shares, but samples of all that is eaten are preserved to be offered to the deity later on. Not all of this is actually offered, enough having been kept back to provide a ritual communal participation of the residue after the offering had been made. In Sierra Leone, at the end of the *Nyɔlɛ* ceremony of the *Awujoh* feast, when the food which had been set aside is offered to the ancestors, all the participants scramble for what is left in the bowl. One has to be present at the ceremony to experience how this scramble for the remnant does indeed produce in the participants a fellow-feeling based on a fellow-participation of the food with the ancestors. In some cases, the ancestors are symbolized and assumed to be present. Thus among the *Mende* of Sierra Leone, the little hut-shaped black ant-hills that

38

dot the countryside are sometimes brought into the shrine in which the offering is made because the ants which live in them are thought to be analogous to the dead: they live in what is a good replica of the round huts in which the ancestors used to live and they borrow from the earth and are not ordinarily visible to onlookers.[52] Jomo Kenyatta however claims that the *Kikuyu*[53] do not worship their ancestors. He prefers the term 'communion with ancestors' instead of 'ancestor worship'. So in his opinion 'the ceremony of communing with ancestral spirits . . . brings back to him (the African participant) the memory and glory of his forefathers'. He therefore draws a distinction between 'the ceremonies of communion with the ancestors' spirits' and 'those directed to the Supreme Being'. He goes on to say 'The words "prayer" and "worship" . . . are never used in dealing with the ancestors' spirits. These words are reserved for solemn rituals and sacrifices directed to the power of the unseen.' Accordingly when, say, 'a sheep is sacrificed to them', this is a gift; and what may 'seem to an outsider to be prayers directed to the ancestors, are nothing but the tributes symbolizing the gifts which the elders would have received had they been alive, and which the living elders now receive.' When therefore a family disaster is diagnosed by a diviner as caused by the fact that the spirits of the ancestors are angry and a feast is arranged, 'the spirits so offended would be invited and offered the feast, and asked to communicate with and resume friendly relations with the living family or individuals.'[54] According to Dr. Idowu, the sacrifices offered at Yoruba funeral ceremonies, constitute a covenant with the dead.[55]

On close examination of the totemic concept, we find that it has factors common to that of the Ancestral relations and therefore the totem is ontologically no different from the spirits of the ancestors. A person dies and, normally, his memory perishes. The African situation proves very congenial to this attitude because without the records of deaths, the date would go out of easy recall and in the absence of communal records, little can be preserved of the daring exploits of the men who were of social influence. The warriors and heroic hunters who risked their lives for the preservation of their communes; the natural parents to whom men owed their birth and upbringing; these all run the risk of social dissolution after death.

To overcome this communal disadvantage, the primitive African transforms them all into parents and so preserves, in terms of spirit behaviour, the general attitudes and influences which are attributed to parents. Tree and animal, warrior and parent are preserved in the single idiom of ancestor. Ancestral origins can of course be treated to a point beyond which human memory can never penetrate; so they become metaphysical entities. The historic situation is translated into meta-history thus representing some action done *in illo tempore* as Eliade would say by some archetypal parent. Such archetypes are however the mental creations of primitive man i.e. in the African situation, of the primitive African. They are designed to account for every event contingent with the day to day experiences of life. This is the basis of the African's interpretation of 'Reality'. The conjured mental creations come to be understood as endowed with intelligence and the capacity to exert force. Thus the ancestral spirits direct the behaviour of the community and the totemic spirits ensure that the mores are not violated.

The question must now be asked 'What is the real significance of the Dogma of super-size'? Since all dogmas are built on myth, we would say that it provides an answer to some of the puzzling situations of life in which the 'real African' has found himself. He sees in the unusual features of life, manifestations of the sacred, an 'exterior force that differentiates it from its *milieu* and gives it meaning and life.'[56] He naturally believes in a Supreme Being but his belief undergoes stages of valuation and re-valuation all the more so because the Supreme Being is not demonstrable, nor is He of easy access to mankind. In particular, the primitive African suffers from many discomforts which Nature imposes upon him. Why, for example, does a woman bear twins or triplets instead of the normal sibling, and so seem to reflect the life that belongs to the lower animals most of which produce a litter at parturition? Add to this the fact that such births are accompanied by excessive pains and the social and economic difficulties that come of rearing them. Why does the human male hanker after a woman to the extent that he feels that he could not live apart from her? Or again, why does an owl unlike most other birds not only feed on rats and other small animals, but also fly about at night when most other living animals are asleep? A similar question could be asked of the bat. Indeed the features of a bat do suggest its unique difference. In Sierra Leone, the Mendes refer to a bat as *gbavε–ñoima*, short for *gbave-ñonima*, which we would interpret to mean 'by way of difference from a bird', and so 'a bird with a difference, neither beast nor bird'. The bat has a mouse-like face. The chameleon and the stick-insect manifest distinctive qualities which make them unique but also make them suggestive of human discomfort and disabilities. The child weakened by a wasting disease with its ribs protruding out of its sides and the motionless corpse of a near relation respectively seem to reflect the known characteristics of the chameleon and the stick-insect respectively. Here we might do well to recall Carl Jung's definition of a Symbol as 'the best possible description, or formula, of a relatively unknown fact; a fact however, which is none the less recognised or postulated as existing.'[57] Modern scientific thinking adopts different categories to express the notion of casuality. To traditional man however, these modes of thought are quite foreign. He thinks in terms of a system of cause and effect which is of a non-physical nature. Fr. Placide Tempels writing of the Baluba of the Congo states that they hold a dynamic concept of 'being' i.e. 'being' is to them 'that which possesses force.'[58] We would go on to say that the other West African tribes we have studied also understand 'being' in terms of vital force. This force may be expressed by 'the word' of human beings, as in the case of the *Boh* Cult; it may be strengthened by the superior force of another being higher in the scale of existence as when the stub of a firewood is talked to by a farmer and it becomes the guardian of his farm or as in the case of *Shigidi*. Equally so the manes of a near or distant relative may influence the stick-insect to enter a house. The force may also be lessened by the evil influence of a hostile, foreign force. Thus an evil spirit is alleged to be responsible for causing the wasting disease of the child who suffers from the so-called chameleon disease because of the primary assumption that the chameleon is different in its appearance and its habits from other animals of its size.[59] In the same way, a woman having her menses expends the vital force, blood, and therefore diminishes her vital force. This diminution of vital force is thought to be a debilitating condition and therefore suggestive of illness and death, to males. To the Akan it is even destructive of the vital force present in gold, so they would therefore not permit such a dangerous influence near the site of a gold mine.[60] Again, human blood possesses a greater vitality than that of members of the vegetable kingdom because man is the crown of creation. So the Temnes believe that the loss of that vital force would destroy the vital force which makes crops bear fruit. Sexual intercourse as was noted earlier, has a debilitating effect on the participants and therefore diminishes their vital force within a period of time following the act. So those who take part in the sex act will have a diminishing effect on the vital force of the spirits of a shrine, as in Ghana;[61] among the Temnes of Sierra Leone, contact between them and a newly circumcised person will, it is believed, reduce the power of the force which makes for the early healing of the wound.

With regard to the ancestors, their spirits are the most powerful next to God as vital forces. So also the totems are regarded with considerable awe and reverence because they either represent the spirits of the founding fathers, as for example, among the Kwotto of Nigeria, or are the incarnation of the Akan deities (the *abosam*).[62]

We would therefore say that the Dogma of Super-Size is an essential element of the notions of ontology found among primitive Africans, who see in their various situations, evidences of vital forces which provide a theory of causality unknown to Western scientific laws. These vital forces are however within the divine plan for the world.

ANCESTOR WORSHIP

A Discussion of Some of the Problems Inherent in the Phrase

1. THE MECHANICS

The phrase 'ancestor-worship' has now become so hallowed by time, that any attempt to examine it must encounter serious difficulties because of the traditional interpretation given to the practice. These difficulties manifest themselves either in the forthright suggestion that this is abominable idolatory or in a denial that real worship takes place. Even when one can resolve these attitudes, the question is further confused by the suggestion that the ancestors in fact appear to their descendants in dreams and express their feelings accordingly. Basic to this latter notion, of course, is the major suggestion that the ancestors, now in the spirit life, feel and react in forms identical with their previous human natural behaviour. Talking to students from various parts of West Africa, one is at first surprised to note that they believe that the ancestors come by their bed-side and talk to them during their sleep and this in fact explains why they, more often, dream of their parents scolding them, complaining of neglect and, less so, of the parents congratulating them on their successes. Of course some ancestors are said to have *come* in dreams to prescribe certain medical herbs to their descendants in times of illness.[1] This is an aspect of the ancestors which needs a separate discussion. In this article, we shall concentrate on a discussion of the ancestors with special reference to the role they are supposed to play in the general life of the community.

In the first place, the ancestors seem to fall into several categories, some of which naturally overlap, but which for the purposes of clarity and convenience may be set out as follows:

(a) direct genealogical ancestors of a particular family or groups of families – grandfathers, grandmothers, fathers, mothers, uncles, aunts, and the various in-law-combinations produced by marriage.

43

(b) The communal national heroes whose memories have come down in history as the defenders of their town or village, and of their tribe. Here the major tribal cults e.g. in Mende-land, Poro and Sande, are prominent. They are the founding fathers from whose life-blood the existence of the community was derived and on which it continues to be sustained with the aid of the contemporary leaders.

(c) Ancestors associated with professional expertise – hunters, sailors, priests of a particular cult; farmers who had worked a particular plot of ground. These have acquired importance in view of their familiarity with the practice of a particular art or special skills.

(d) Ancestors associated with a particular sacred spot e.g. those who prayed together at a particular shrine, and are supposed to have acquired the liturgical techniques demanded at such shrines and to be able to participate in them.

These four main varieties naturally overlap because the founding fathers may be rightly expected to play the role of group (d) at the sacred sites of the secret societies and must also, at one time or another, have been parents of their own children as shown in (a). So too farmers would include those under group (a) and might be included under group (b).

(e) The Mende also have an amorphous group who when alive were of migratory tendencies and never really belonged to the family hearth or to the village or town. These go by the name *ngɛlɛpeleihuyafanga* – spirits who stop by the way-side.[2]

The direct active influence of the ancestors on their descendants is however in inverse proportion to the date of their death. That is to say, that the longer the interval after their death, the vaguer their memory becomes, and their direct authority accordingly wanes. At the same time, they are supposed to acquire progressively, a super-vening control of the contemporary situation because they are now nearer God. Thus the Mende for example, talk of the *Kɛkɛni*, the fathers, whose memories are relatively fresh, and the *Ndeblaa* the forebears, who are virtually forgotten but are nevertheless a moral force in their communities. The *Kɛkɛni* are generally assumed to be in close contact with the everyday affairs of life and understand what, one might be tempted to say, constitute the contemporary situation. The *Ndeblaa* on the other hand, although they are understood to have maintained their human qualities, yet they are thought to be much more *spirit* and so more distant from their descendants. They are conceived of as proximate to *ŋgewɔ*, and are often referred to

44

as being in the arms of ŋgewɔ. The following prayer is instructive on this point.

'A ŋgewɔ, Kenɛi Mɔmɔ, i hiti bi ma; i hiti Nduawo ma; i hiti Nbeblaa kpɛlɛ ma ti bi yaka hu' i.e. O God let it (our prayers) reach you, Kenɛi Mɔmɔ; let it reach Nduawo; let it reach all our forefathers who are in your bosom (i.e. by your side).[3]

This proximation indeed makes one wonder how far the ancestors at the Ndeblaa stage have reached veneration close to that accorded to ŋgewɔ. The spirits who stop by the way-side are however never forgotten. At national festivals, some food is usually scattered along the main roads leading to a town, to provide for their needs. They must never be neglected. So also, possibly hostile ones are provided for and arc not allowed good cause to vent any malice.

Among the Sierra Leone Creoles, a similar though not identical situation exists. At an Awujoh festival, an old female member, preferably the oldest, of the family is generally the first to invoke the spirits, presumably, because she has the longest contact and the farthest memory of the family line. But even she ends her invocations with a blanket phrase like 'ɔl dɛn wan we wi nɔ no', i.e. '(you) all (the rest) whom we do not know – and can no longer recall.' The spirits are credited with the capacity for discerning truth – 'una we de na tru wɔl' i.e. 'you who live in the world of truth and do discern truth and are therefore no longer subject to the effects of deception.' In spite of the long Christian tradition, or perhaps because of it, the Creole ancestors are thought to be close to God. One would say here that the two lines of pagan belief and Christian teaching seemed to have crossed and the distinctions have become completely blurred.

At this point, the nature of the rite which takes place when the ancestors are invoked calls for careful analysis. Both among the Mende and the Creoles whom we have already mentioned, the rites involve the offering of food and the offer of prayers mainly petitions.[4] In both cases, food is offered, water is presented, (among the Mende twice, the first time for the ancestors to wash their hands) and by both groups for the ancestors to drink, as after a meal, followed by a little alcohol (usually palm wine among the Mende). The prayers then follow. It is not easy to be categorical about the end-point of the prayers but the evidence suggests that the ancestors are expected to make the required responses.

The following sample prayers will illustrate the points we have mentioned.

2. PRAYERS

(a) Creole Prayer – *This was the first in a series of five.*
The spokesman was the eldest woman member of the family present.
Other members spoke later in order of their seniority – in translation from Krio – recorded at an *Awujoh* Festival on April 27, 1963, in Freetown by the writer. *(The Awujoh was arranged to inform the ancestors that the eldest son of the family was about to get married.)*
'Grandma X, Papa Y, Uncle B, you all who have gone, see what a great occasion this is (coming). Here is cold water, drink. (*She pours this in a hole prepared for the offering*). Here are your grandchildren and great grandchildren. See to it that everything takes place by the power of God. Look at H, the whole family, the grandchildren and the great-grandchildren. Guide us all – all of us. Here is your cold water (*she pours more water*) to gladden your hearts. Pray for us, you all who have gone before. Here is D. Look upon us all here present, and those who (of the family) are not able to be here with us. You know us all in the spirit (being spirit). M is at her own home, please do not forget her; Z, M's husband is overseas, he is your grand-son-in-law, son-in-law etc., Take good care of him, don't leave (neglect) him, by the power of God. Here is food for you all, bean-cake (ground and fried), boiled beans, fried plantains, rice, the leg of a chicken, wing, a foot etc., (*She places these in the hole*). Open their way, (i.e. grant them success), by the power of God.'

(b) A Mende Prayer recorded by Dr. S. Hofstra in 1934 at a ceremony associated with the Oil Palm fruit.
(*The food offered consisted of rice, palm-oil, and rats.*) *The leader of the participants* addresses the spirits of successful climbers as follows, while preparing the food – i.e. getting it ready for the sacrifice, '*Bindipaamea*, (name of a once skilful climber), you once danced on the oil palms, *Suakata, Momodugba, Blamagome, Kpɔlubahu* and *Gɔmaluvandɔlɛ* (*names of other famous climbers*), let this (food) reach you; let it (also) reach *Kplubahu*; long ago you cut palm-fruits. Therefore I came last night and said a prayer, so that nobody may fall from the tree; let them not die. See that no snake bites a person in the tree and that no thorn cuts him; our lives depend on it. We therefore make its (the tree's) heart cool and give it this pot; let the whole of it reach the tree. May the climbers not slip from the oil-palm, let them not fall, let them not die. Let no danger fall on us. This is the rice. I'm going'. (*Then rice served on a banana leaf is laid at the foot of the tree*). 'This was the word we all spoke. We shall not again give you a gift during this dry season. All our companions have,

but we here have not yet offered you our gift. This is a large, mighty pot'. (*Some rice is laid on the leaf a second time and nearby, are placed a strip of white cloth and the leaves used for Poro ndimɔi. Some rice is placed on the road for the less sociable ndimanyoyafangaa*). Water is poured three times over the rice near the foot of the tree with the words, 'Wash your hands' and soon afterwards by which time the spirits should have finished their meal, (*he again pours water*), saying, You ate the rice, now wash your hands'.[5]

At the end of these prayers, again taking the Mende and Creoles as examples, the response is usually '*bai God pauer*', 'by the power of God', (Creole) and among the Mende, '*ŋgewɔ jahun*', i.e. 'by the Will of God'. This suggests that the ancestors are thought of as capable of fulfilling the requests expressed in the petitions, but also somewhat dependent in the ultimate analysis on the sovereign Will of God, who has greater power than the ancestors (human beings now spirit), and controls all that happens in the world. But judging from the prayers we have cited above, the ancestors seem to form a chain linking the oldest-fathers and mothers to their descendants. Every care must therefore be taken by the living not to miss out any link in this chain.

3. TYPES OF ANCESTRAL RITES

The ancestral rites also fall under several categories, again, not altogether exclusive of each other.

(1) Good-will offerings:

(a) often merely celebrating the death of an individual e.g. on the third, the seventh and fortieth day after a death.[6]
(b) Sometimes commemorating the anniversary of a death.
(c) At other times, the offering is designed to invoke the support of the ancestors for some venture to be taken by a member of the family e.g. his or her getting married, or going away from home. The Mende tribal heroes are commemorated at annual festivals.

(2) Thank-offerings for the assumed contributions of the ancestors towards the success or recovery from a severe illness of a member of the family.

(3) Propitiatory-offerings:

When a member or a friend of the family dreams of a deceased ancestor who complains of being hungry, (i.e. neglected), or when a disaster (personal or national) occurs or in cases of illness – for example, the *Boro-ma-Sar* rite among the Temne of Sierra Leone. At this rite, the heroes of the area are invoked if there is, say, a fall in the catch of fish in a fishing area, or even a plague of mosquitoes. The Mende propitiate their national heroes at annual festivals by the rivers along which a town lies, as in (1), (c).

(4) Mediatory-offerings – as among the Mende when the *Ndeblaa* are requested to pass on the petitions of the river-spirits to pacify them, so that voyagers or fishermen or swimmers are not drowned in a river, or to (the spirit of) the palm-tree, as in our sample prayer B.

Here a dual intention seems to be implied. The (spirit of the) palm-tree or the river-spirits are in fact the goal of the petitions for safety but only the *Ndeblaa* can readily reach them. So they are first invoked and then requested to pass on the petitions for safety. Among the Kwotto of Nigeria the spirits of the Ancestor-Kings are generally invoked to ask God to send rain and those of ordinary men to request health for the children, strength and success for the men and babies for the women.[7] The Creole *Awujoh* feast serves all the above-mentioned purposes, depending on the prevailing circumstances. Basic to all these rites are the provision of choice food, such as one would prepare for one's parents, although rather incongruously, special care is also taken to include in the offering representative bits of everything either to be eaten or already eaten (as the rite demands) by the offerers. Thus the Mende offer rice and stew of game flesh hunted specially for certain occasions, or as in the case of the Oil-palm ceremony referred to above, palm-tree rats which are difficult to trap. Most times a chicken is cooked in addition, and its gizzard cut into small pieces and included in the offering. The Creole *Awujoh* offering includes the best portions of a chicken but also the wings and feet which normally only children eat. They do not however make a point of offering the gizzard as the Mende do.

4. THE RAISON D'ETRE OF THE RITES

We may now attempt an analysis of the purpose of the rites viz: the maintenance of a community spirit of harmony. In every case where food is offered to the ancestors, more food than is required for the offering is cooked so that all the participants may share in it. In some of the Mende river-ceremonies, a whole village participate in the rite, (every able-bodied male having first been required to share in the hunt), the participants usually eating their own portions after the ancestors have been first served. Among the Creole, the food is cooked early in the day and the participants then have a meal. Later in the afternoon, often by 6.00 p.m., the offering is made. All the participants gather round the hole into which the food is to be placed and when the offering is completed, there is a communal scramble for the rest. The act is thus communal in *intent* and *effect*.

This communal aspect is seen both in the preparatory notice given to the spirits advising them of the date of the rites, so that they can all foregather at one spot, and in the turn-out of the whole village or of the family and their friends. The rites therefore bring together the total extended family of ancestors and their descendants at a common meal.[8]

In other words *harmony* between the living and the dead, and among the living is a paramount consideration.[9] A communal meal is usually the end-rite of the Mende secret societies. Among the Creoles all petty quarrels among the relatives or friends of the family are settled during an *Awujoh* feast. The spirits are not to be given cause to be 'angry' nor must their descendants harbour a grievance against each other.

This desire to preserve peace and goodwill explains the Mende practice of giving some of the food offered at the rites, especially so of a national nature, to the roving spirits who in their life-time did not settle at any one place, and to possibly ill-disposed ones.

This desire for *harmony* lies behind the offer of water and alcoholic spirits. Both are referred to as *cold water* by the Mende; the Creoles refer to alcoholic spirits as *hɔtɛ-hɔti* even though they do have the temperature of the time of day, and in some cases would be (to us) much too warm to be palatable, But water is used to cultivate *harmony*. Among the Creoles, a newly married couple are given water to drink from the same glass. Two glasses full of water are in fact used but each is switched over, one first to the bridegroom then to the bride, and vice-versa. To have drunk water from the same glass is to covenant not to have any secrets which must be held back from one's co-participants. Water in general *cools* and *refreshes* one who is tired and thirsty; but it is also the simplest and most acceptable manifestation of hospitality. A Creole describing how inhospitable a person is, would say 'Not even (a drop of) water did he give to me'. To refuse a request for water from a stranger is a social offence to the Creole. Similar ideas exist among the Mende. In other words, the offer of *cold water*, (i.e. a drink), is intended to *cool* the (possible) anger of the ancestors and to dispose them to listening to the petitions. This desire for a *cool* heart[10] explains why the Mende avoid adding pepper to any food to be offered to the Ancestors. Pepper chokes and irritates those who include much of it in their food.

49

Although the Creoles on the other hand, add a lot of pepper to the *Awujoh* meals served to ordinary consumers they usually take out that quantity of the boiled beans (black-eyed ones) which would later be offered to the ancestors. The rest of the food tends to be highly peppered. Thus we may go on to say that the offerings to the ancestors are intended to build up a spirit of reconciliation or conciliation, as circumstances demand. We however have yet to answer the question Is Ancestor-Worship, true Worship?

5. THE RATIONALE

Devotees of the monotheistic religions, Judaism, Christianity and Islam associate the term *Worship*, exclusively to their attitude towards the Supreme God – Yahweh, God, the Father, Son and Holy Ghost, and Allah respectively. In Africa, even though the Supreme God is said to be worshipped somewhat by a few groups – the Kaffirs, the Kikuyu, the Kposso, the Yoruba, the Ewe and the Akan – there is little extant evidence of any organised cults, with shrines and priests, dedicated to the Supreme God. On the other hand, it does seem as if there is some definite pattern in the rituals used for both ancestor worship and other forms of cultic worship. The question however arises as to the propriety of the term worship in the rites, such as we described above. One is inclined to say that there seem to be the makings of a Liturgy with a definite shape in these rites. Dr. Idowu of the University of Ibadan, a Methodist minister, has called our attention to the existence of Yoruba liturgies which have been preserved 'almost undisturbed for generations' because of the correctness of their conduct. 'In Yoruba (cultic) worship, there is nothing of the nonconformists' go-as-you-please style'[11] – Dr. Idowu would of course say that these liturgies are used in the worship of the divinities, but as T.F. Fabiyi has pointed out[12] the many *orisas* of Yorubaland may be traced to deified ancestors. Dr. Idowu himself has observed the *Oduduwa* and *Sango*[13] were deified heroes. So even the Yoruba divinities give us some basis for the study of Ancestor Worship. The due performance of the Yoruba liturgies calls for special qualities in the worshippers. First of all, they must be ritually clean. This may mean the avoidance of sexual intercourse immediately before worship or making sure of a 'thorough washing' afterwards, carrying 'bad medicine' on one's person, or worst of all having an 'impure heart'. Secondly, the rites are performed in the shrine of the god. The worshippers generally salute the god and acknowledge his providential care; a libation of water is poured. The

50

worshippers then make their petitions and determine the divining with kola-nuts the attitude of the god to their worship, and of their future prospects. When a priest is present, he blesses the participants at the end of the rites. The petitions made are for 'material blessing'. 'Protection from sickness and death, gifts of longevity, children, prosperity in enterprises, victory over enemies, protection from evil spirits and of relatives near and distant, rectification of unhappy destinies, and abundant provision of material things; blessings on all well-wishers and damnation on all ill-wishers.'[14] In essence these forms of worship are closely similar to those we described in our previous study.

Dr. Idowu however has something to say of Ancestor Worship specifically. He observes that the Yoruba rarely say 'I am going to speak to the "spirit" of my father; what they say is "I am going to speak to my father"'. He therefore infers that 'Ancestor Worship' is a wrong nomenclature for that which in fact is no 'worship' but a manifestation of an unbroken family relationship between deceased parents and their living descendants.[15] This comment deserves some attention because it seems to hold the clue to much of what we shall have to say on the subject. W.C. Willoughby has also suggested that the discarnate spirits of the ancestors are addressed 'in much the same terms' as if they were in the flesh.[16] Again, Jomo Kenyatta prefers the phrase 'communion with the ancestors' to 'ancestor worship'. He states that 'the words "prayer" and "worship" . . . are never used in dealing with the ancestors' spirits. These words are reserved for solemn rituals and sacrifices directed to the power of the unseen'. He goes on to say, when 'a sheep is sacrificed' to the ancestors, this is a 'gift'; and what may 'seem to an outsider to be prayers directed to the ancestors, are nothing but the tributes symbolizing the gifts which the elders would have received had they been alive, and which the living elders now receive'. When therefore a family disaster is diagnosed by a diviner as caused by the fact that the spirits of the ancestors are angry and a feast is arranged, 'the spirits so offended would be invited and offered the feast and asked to communicate with and resume friendly relations with the living family or individuals'.[17] Jomo Kenyatta elsewhere points out the linguistic differences in the phrases for Deity worship 'and' communion with the ancestors. The Kikuyu expression for the former means literally 'to beseech Ngai or to worship Ngai', and that for the latter, 'to pour out or sprinkle beer for the spirits'. When on ceremonial occasions both beer and an animal are offered, the language used literally means 'to slaughter and to pour out beer for the spirits'. Here the distinction is quite specific. The Kikuyu 'beseech' or 'worship' *Ngai*, but they offer gifts to the ancestors; for the private individual this consists of pouring out a little of whatever one is drinking, on to the ground for the ancestors, and, at the communal level, 'a special quantity of beer brewed for presentation to the ancestors 'as well as the slaughter of a beast.[18] It is important also to note that when all is well with the community, it is taken for granted that *Ngai* is pleased with the general behaviour of the people and no prayers need be offered to Him. He 'must not be needlessly pestered'. Indeed the prayers offered to *Ngai* are strictly petitions for 'rain and a good harvest'; 'health and peace'.

A sacrifice is offered to *Ngai* on serious occasions like drought or an outbreak of an epidemic or a serious illness.[19] At the birth, initiation, marriage and death of every Kikuyu, the whole family establish contact with *Ngai* on his behalf. But these four crises apart, there seems to be no contact at the level of the Individual with *Ngai*. Other crises are referred to the ancestors, e.g. the violation of a taboo,[20] and illness or injury,[21] with the help of a diviner. Monica Wilson also says of *Nyakyusa* sacrifices that 'the conclusion that this, (i.e. the sacrifice), is a communion between the living and the dead is inescapable'.[22] They worship the now deified hero ancestors also designated as creators, but the dominant theme in their rituals and more so in the rituals celebrated by private persons is their kinship ties.[23]

At a typical sacrificial rite they pray:
   'May the children sleep, may we all sleep, may it rain, may there be much food, may milk be plentiful.'
'Then follows a communion in which young "grand children" of the dead share of the sacred meat and beer. The shades eat together . . .'[24]
Another prayer reads *inter alia*, 'We pray to Kyala.
   May theft go away. Give us food and beans and millet, may we eat and be satisfied . . . .'[25]
One factor which seems to determine Nyakusa worship is the 'anger' of the ancestors. For the Nyakyusa, 'harmony' is a desideratum; and this holds true both in relation to the living members with kinship ties, or with the living *vis-a-vis* the dead.[26]

We may say here that for the Nyakyusa as for the Yoruba, good healthy personal relationships are essential for the proper ordering of the sacrifices. We may pause and note that Dr. Idowu is prepared to use the phrase Hero-worship. But does he mean by this term, the attitude of a young adolescent to an older person he admires? The reference to *Oduduwa* and *Sango* is to deified ancestors. The communion he refers to must therefore be regarded as not merely a reference to social contacts.

Ulli Beier on the other hand specifically asserts that the Yoruba 'worship their ancestors', and adds that the pagan Yoruba attributes misfortune to an angered ancestor. In cases of disputes which cannot be easily resolved, the contestants will go to the tomb of an ancestor, offer prayer and sacrifices. 'Then they will evoke his spirit and take an oath: "May the one who has not spoken the truth in this matter die within seven days – or some such formula. The Yoruba will remember his ancestors at every meal, and he will never fail to pour a libation to them".'[27] Writers on the Akan of Ghana in West Africa, either explicitly use the phrase 'worship of the ancestors' (so Busia),[28] or talk of the propitiation of the ancestral spirits (so Rattray, Meyerowitz).[29] In any case, offerings are made to them; they are propitiated; their aid is invoked in times of crises and on Festivals like the Adae. Rattray tells us that 'the predominant influences in the Ashanti religion are neither 'Saturday Sky-god' nor 'Thursday Earth-goddess' nor even the hundreds of gods (*abosom*), with which it is true the land is filled, but are the *samanfo*, the spirits of the departed forbears of the clan'.[30] So indeed 'before partaking of wine or spirits', 'the Ashanti pours a little on the ground from the cup . . . for the shades of his ancestors'.[31]

Busia has recorded some details of an Adwera Festival at Wenchi, which may be useful in this discussion. On the first night, Tuesday, the women sang 'songs of thanksgiving' to the gods, the Supreme Being and to the ancestors for the gift of a good harvest, for life and children, or prayers for the same things. Or the following day (Wednesday), the chief spokesman of the district (*Ɔkyeame*) poured libations of rum and offered as sacrifice a sheep provided by the chief. At the libations, he mentioned each of the reigning chief's predecessors by name, saying 'Here is drink' (*as he pours the libations*) or here is meat (*as he offered the meat*). All of you, grandsires, by your help the year has come round again; your grandson (the chief) has come this morning to bring you a sheep and drink; grant him health; prosperity to the Wenchi people; let the celebrations about to begin pass peacefully. Blessing, blessing'. On the Monday of the second week, the central rite was performed. A procession consisting of women carrying food in brasspans, a row of boys carrying palm-wine and locally brewed beer from maize corn; the chief's own mother, the queen-mother and other senior women of the royal families in the town. They all proceeded to a sacred tree. Two bearers brought water from a nearby tree. Seated beneath the tree, the chief's mother offered the food and the drink. Mentioning each departed chief and then each queen-mother by name and saying, 'Here is food (or drink, *as is appropriate*); all of you receive this and eat (or drink); the year has come round again; today we celebrate it; bring us blessing; blessing to the chief who sits on your stool; health to the people; let women bear children; let the men prosper in their undertakings; life to all; we thank you for the good harvest, for standing behind us. Blessing, blessing, blessing. The attendant crowd reply: 'Blessing, blessing, blessing.'[32] This type of prayer is typical of those offered by the Yorubas. Dr. Idowu describes them as having an 'objective petitionary character'.[33]

In Sierra Leone, one comes across similar prayers to the dead among the Creole, the Temne and the Mende, for example – the occasions ranging from individual to national crises, happy occasions like marriage (among the Creole) or initiation ceremonies at the end of *Poro* among the Mende or commemorations of a death.

The general impression gained from a study of the prayers offered to the ancestors is that they do not differ intrinsically from the prayers offered by the Kikuyu to *Ngai*. Even Jomo Kenyatta admits that the Kikuyu 'expect *Mwange-Nyaga* to answer their prayers favourably in return for the present given', i.e. the animal sacrifice. This law of 'give and take' governs the prayers to the ancestors which we have cited above. Again, he states that when a person falls ill and is directed by a diviner to communicate with the spirit of an offended ancestor who is thought to have caused the illness, 'Atonement is made and the invalid recovers'.[34] Of course, when this treatment fails, an approach is made to *Ngai*, jointly by the ancestors and the living members of the family concerned. Jomo Kenyatta also mentions one other instance of appeal by the body of living and dead members of a family. This is in respect of a person who has been struck by lightning. What is significant here is that such a victim is generally thought to have been daring to look upwards (during a thunder storm) to see *Mwene-Nyaga* stretching himself and cracking his joints in readiness for his active service to chase away or smash his enemies'.[35] We can see no difference between *propitiating* a god, and *making atonement with an ancestor* as far as intention goes. One common factor that is prominent in the two types of Kikuyu rites, is *anger*, referred to as the anger of the ancestor,[36] on the one hand, and the wrath of *Ngai* on the other. The first is described as calling for atonement, the second for propitiation, both producing the same effect – the restoration of good relations between the parties, i.e., *Communication*.

We would therefore suggest that Jomo Kenyatta has drawn a distinction between the two actions, but a distinction without a difference. The law of 'give and take' which determines Kikuyu worship of *Ngai* also operates in the prayers to the ancestors cited above from West Africa and operates in the language implied in the so-called Kikuyu 'communion with the ancestors'.[37] We must also note that the Nuer, according to Evans-Pritchard, seem to direct their prayers to God although they recognise certain spirits of the air and of the earth, as well as spirits of their ancestors. These are distinct spirits, but Being Spirit, they are all children of God or refractions of his hypostasis.[38] So whilst it can be said that prayers are offered to the spirits, it is also held that these prayers are offered to God. At the same time, samples of these prayers show the same structure as those already cited, e.g.:

'Our father, it is thy universe, it is thy will, let us be at peace, let the souls of the people be cool, thou art our father, remove all evil from our path.'[39]

As Evans-Pritchard himself rightly observes, 'They are asking God for deliverance from evil, so that they may have peace, denoted by a variety of images with emotional and ideational relatedness – sleep, lightness, ease, coolness, softness, prayer, the domestic hearth, abundant life, and life as it should be according to the nature of the person.'[40] We would therefore maintain that Africans do offer prayers to their ancestors and for the purpose of this work, such prayers constitute a form of worship. Even Dr. Idowu says without any qualification, that to the Yoruba, 'Egungun designates the spirit of the deceased to which *worship* (italics mine), is offered at the ancestral shrine'.[41] We may therefore summarise the present discussion so far by saying that Africans do worship their ancestors as they do their divinities. This worship consists of prayers, sacrifices, and divination on communal occasions or prayers and divinations on private occasions. In the latter case, a priest may or not be present, although it would be correct to think of the owner of a personal deity as its private priest. All such forms of worship are built around certain ritual acts, which themselves demand certain preliminary requirements of priest and worshippers, e.g. 'a pure heart' towards one's kinsmen among the Neuer, and the Yoruba. The Yoruba rites also demand an intermission of the sex-act before the day of the performance of the rite and abjure an impure heart. The prayers themselves consist of petitions related to the welfare of the worshippers, their children, their harvests, peace and goodwill in the country. Dare we say that these rites we have been discussing do not constitute worship?

THE AFRICAN CONCEPT OF DEATH

Human life, for Africans as for all other human beings, revolves around four major events – birth, puberty, marriage, and death. Jomo Kenyatta refers to them as crises, which affect not only an individual Kikuyu but also the whole family and its neighbours and friends.[1] Typical of this attitude is the convention of the Krio of Sierra Leone, which demands that at the birth of a child, it is very bad taste for relatives and neighbours not to congratulate the new mother and wish the baby well, with a gift however small as a symbol of good-will. Not to do so suggests grievous hostility and ill-will; it is an unpardonable social offence. Among the Mende, also of Sierra Leone, everyone living near the home of a newly born baby must wish him well – *fia-le, O* ('may all go well with you'). At the birth of twins and triplets, this good-will is given practical expression. The women of the neighbourhood take the twins, displayed in a winnowing fan, and go dancing with them from house to house, where they are given presents of goods or clothing. Kenyatta also tells that if a man is struck by lightning – a punishment for looking up when it is flashing – but not killed, his family must come together to plead corporately on his behalf with *Mwena Nyaga* or *Ngai*, the God of the Kikuyu who ordinarily is not to be bothered. Both the living and dead members of the family are believed to join in propitiating the anger of *Ngai*.[2]

Other instances of family solidarity abound in Africa. However, we shall restrict the rest of this chapter primarily to some West African tribes.

1. BIRTH AND DEATH

Of the four major life events mentioned earlier, birth and death constitute the first and last. At birth, the baby is separated from the

56

mother and assumes a new mode of existence; at death, both the newly born and the centenarian cease to exist and are parted from the larger group of living beings. In cases of still-birth, the baby is born dead. There thus exists a close relationship between these two poles of man's life.

According to Dr. J.B. Danquah, in Akan thought the true contrast is between *birth* and death, not between *life* and death. He goes on to suggest that the words death and life must be thought of in terms of one's whole outlook on life. For a selfish man, living 'for himself alone', death is a reality. But for an individual who is aware of his belonging to a larger whole death is 'nothing but a stage in the consciousness of race, the experience of his kind'. For such, 'Death is only an aspect of birth, . . . an instrument of the total destiny, the continuity of the kind, the permanence and persistence of the organic whole which is the greatest good of endeavour'. Indeed, he adds, 'nothing lives or dies of itself'.[3]

Danquah assumes that a man is born with a destiny which is to be fulfilled by means of successive reincarnations. At the same time, the blood of his race runs through his veins and therefore from him to his descendants. Death is thus 'less than a negation of life'[4] because 'the fact of family carries with it an assurance of continuity, its endurance, persistence, and permanence'.[5] Danquah's language is often difficult to understand. The reincarnations no doubt come to an end when the destiny assigned to a man at birth is fulfilled.[6] But by that time his descendants have come into their own, and the cycle continues at a different level. Death is of course biologically a new thing, a consequence of 'the failure of the higher animals and man to integrate perfectly the vital energy put forth by them with the mental development' they had attained. For the good Akan Chief, Danquah adds, death is the road to deification.[7]

The Yoruba of Nigeria and the Krio of Sierra Leone also believe in reincarnations, and maintain that when people die, they return to this life reincarnate in their descendants. The Yoruba go further than the Krio in postulating successive as well as simultaneous multiple reincarnations. For a man with several children, all of whom showed filial piety in giving him respectable funeral rites, the reincarnation is assumed not only in one grandchild but in several, and in great grandchildren born of the surviving sons, daughters, cousins, and nephews.[8] The Yoruba also hold that a man is born with a destiny (*ori*) which may be requested or assigned to him by *Olodumare* just before he is born. But the idea of the *ori* seems to vacillate between that of something personal and of something belonging to a deceased ancestor. So a man who does not succeed in his undertakings must offer a sacrifice to his *ori*; but a woman may offer a sacrifice to the *ori* of her husband's father, supposedly in heaven. The Mende of Sierra Leone also postulate the predetermined destiny of a man at birth (*nemi*), with the important qualification that the *nemi* blossoms as he performs acts of kindness to others, who in turn utter a word of blessing in their expression of thanks. Presumably, the Mende *nemi* is assumed to be always good, in contrast to the Yoruba *ori* which may be good or bad.[9] The relationship between the destiny of the newly born individual and that of his ancestors is difficult to determine. Danquah's presentation makes this even more difficult, because for him reincarnation takes place only because the destiny of the reincarnate ancestor is as yet unfulfilled. Father Placide Tempels, writing of the Bantu of the Congo, gets over this problem by denying any predetermined destiny of the individual, or of the ancestor whom he presumably reincarnates; instead, he postulates a vital force which brings the newly born individual into a vital relationship with the deceased, who is in a like vital relationship with 'his progenitors'. He goes on to say, 'Perhaps the idea can be better expressed by saying not that it is a predetermined human being belonging to the clan who is reborn, but that it is his individuality returning to take part in the life of the clan by means of the vital influences through which the deceased gives clan individualisation to the living born, to the living fruit of the womb that is to be born into the clan'.[10] Danquah describes this feature as 'racial immortality'.[11] Father Tempels may be right about the vital relationship between the living and the ancestors and between one generation of ancestors and their predecessors, but he has not given enough place to the role ascribed to destiny among the Akan, the Mende, and the Yoruba, for example.

Birth and death in every case remain integrally connected, and even if West Africans do not understand the respective origins of these, they are fairly united in the idea that a baby when born is constituted of body – flesh, blood, bones, and muscles – on the one hand, and spirit on the other. The spirit part comes from the Supreme Being. It is the spark of God, a fire which instills life into the blood of the foetus.[12] The Akan call this spark *Kra*, the Mende *Igafa*, the Yoruba *Emin*. So after a baby is born, when its skin is still soft, each of these tribes allows a set number of days to elapse before it is brought out into the open, in order to give the divine spark – the fire of life – time to take full possession of the body in which it operates. This is another way of keeping the child away from hostile influences, both physical and psychical, which may cause its death.

At death this divine spark returns to its divine origin, and an equal number of days is prescribed for the complete return. The physical properties of the individual – infant or adult – disintegrate, but it seems to be supposed that his individuality remains on earth, continuing its existence in the land of the dead (Akan, *samandow*). So we now find ourselves with two aspects of death – the divine and the personal. The latter is the basis of the belief in the continued existence of the ancestors. They preserve in death their personal likes and dislikes; they feel hungry, become angry, and expect from their children appropriate filial piety and respect; they come to their survivors in dreams; they assume the form of birds, e.g. vultures (the Krio, the Yoruba), or of monkeys and chimpanzees (the Mende). In this context, death is akin to a journey. Among, say the Mende, this journey is up a steep hill, and death gasps are analogous to one's panting for breath when climbing quickly. Some tribes also believe that at death the spirit crosses a river to enter the land of the dead. In some cases, for example among the Yoruba and Mende, these two aspects are not very clearly defined. At the same time, one could say that the good go to the land of the dead – heaven or paradise,[13] while the wicked, generally regarded as witches, are not allowed to survive death. So the Efiks of Calabar (Nigeria) burn witches;[14] the Mende bury them in a shallow grave unmourned and unsung.[15] The Temne used to dismember them and bury their limbs separately. A dead witch is supposed to be much more wicked than a living one, and as a spirit is immune to any anti-witch charms. According to the Akan, even the *Kra* of evil persons are not allowed to stay in the Upper Kingdom, but become evil spirits on earth with the possibility of repentance. If they do repent, they may be reincarnated in children born blind, or lame, or otherwise infirm.[16] Many groups believe that those who die by violence also wander about and sometimes appear to various persons, until their allotted span of life is reached. After that they are able to enter the land of the dead.

Death is symbolically postulated in a number of initiation cults like *poro* among the Mende. *Poro* initiates are said to be eaten by the spirit of the cult at the beginning of the ceremonies and regurgitated in a rebirth at the end.[17] So a Mende man would mention the *hale* (medicine) of which he had died (*has*) as a point of reference when taking a serious oath.

Two associate notions come into view here. The first is that the ancestors live close to God but also close to their living descendants. They intercede with God for them. The Kwotto of Nigeria therefore appeal to their deceased kings to give them rain, i.e., to intercede with God on their behalf for rain, or for relief in times of national disasters. As priest-kings they are now more capable of approaching

God effectively. However, the commoners are not left out; when they die, they are invoked to give strength to the men, babies to the women, and to improve the harvest.[18] It is in this context that the ancestral dead are said, as among the Kroo of Liberia and Sierra Leone, to give children to their descendants.[19] A natural corollary of this notion is that the living descendants are under a moral obligation to maintain sound ethical standards of which the deceased ancestors would approve. It is assumed that the ancestors exercise juridical authority over the living analogous to the authority they wielded during their lifetime. So they mete out punishments when they are neglected, or for misdemeanours on the part of the living. These take various forms: failure in business transactions, sickness, or, as among the Temnes, a poor catch of fish or a plague of mosquitoes. The various rites associated with the offering of sacrifices to the ancestral dead are born of this assumption: the ancestors must be kept happy and pleased with their descendants; otherwise they must be appeased.[20]

The second notion is expressed both negatively and positively. Negatively, it is assumed that because the dead lie in the earth, the earth is corrupt and taboo: it is impregnated with death. Thus the Akan king must not touch the ground with his bare feet or his buttocks, because he must not come near death.[21] Positively, it is felt that since grass and trees spring from the earth, life originates there. These two attitudes blend in the ideas associated with the death of a baby and its assumed return in the birth of its successor. So the Krio, for example, assume that when the first-born in a family dies, it is returned to its mother in a subsequent birth as a joint action of ancestors and the earth.[22] The older generations of the Krio firmly believe that when a baby rolls off its bed, the earth (i.e., the floor of the house) moves up to catch it, and so prevents any serious physical injuries. We may say that the baby's muscles are soft and its bones gelatinous, but the Krio mammy would unremittingly cling to her hallowed understanding of life.

2. DEATH AS AN ENEMY

The death of the young, and particularly of children, is a grievous loss and terrible pain to their families. When, as in the case of families with an Rh blood problem, all babies after the first die in succession, the Yoruba, for example, postulate the existence of a troupe of mischievous spirit-children (*abiku*) who flock together, perhaps under an *iroko* tree, and one or another of them says, 'I go

60

to be born of X, but I will come back', each giving a time – after three months, after ten months, after three years. At the end of the stated period, these babies die and then meet again to revive their childish spirit-folic. The Mende and the Krio hold that the same child keeps on being born and dying. To prevent such successive deaths, mothers give their children talismanic names: the Yoruba and the Krio, *Bamidele*, meaning 'Come, stay in my house', and *Bami-joko*, 'Come sit with me'; the Mende, *Kula haa* – 'Rags', i.e., death clothes; *Lombe*, 'Stay to my benefit'. Chinua Achebe gives a list of such Ibo names: *Onwumbiko*, 'Death, I implore you'; *Ozoemena*, 'May it not happen again'; *Onwuma*, 'Death may please himself'.[23]

Death in action is naturally an enemy, and is often personified, for example among the Temnes. When someone dies, the Ibo of Nigeria run about wildly, slashing at trees and bushes, firing guns in the air, yelling their rage. The Acoli come to a 'funeral – not the immediate burial – fully armed for war. They surround the grave and drive Death away from it with spear and shield', singing at the same time.[24] Although the Yoruba maintain that they scarify the corpses of *abiku* children so they will no longer be welcome among their spirit troupe, it seems truer to say that the scarification is intended to cheat death of a wholesome victim. Cognate with these attitudes is the belief, among the Yoruba for example, that it is a disgrace for a man to die without a male issue.[25] Death signifies a 'process of diminishing strength'.[26] A Temne myth relating to sickness and death confirms this notion. At the same time, man seeks to maintain the stability of his group in the face of the inevitable collapse, one after the other, of the individuals who compose it. Thus funeral rites, whether at the time of death or on a subsequent occasion, provide the group affected an opportunity of being together and becoming 'conscious of itself once again'.[27] The dancing and merriment indulged in by all but the closest relatives also restore this group consciousness and solidarity. They also seem to be intended to limit, and perhaps deny, the destructive powers of death over the group *per se*.[28] The larger a man's family, the bigger and more elaborate his funeral rites. The older he is, the greater the possibilities of mass hysteria during the performances. A man's social and political status also determines the largess provided for the rites. Dancing at funeral rites, like pacemakers for athletes, seems to be designed to give the deceased light feet for his journey to the other world. Dancing may take place on the day of the funeral, as among the Akan,[29] on the third day in the case of a woman, or on the fourth of a man, as among the Mende. Rattray reports that among the Akan, although there is much lamentation from the time of death until the day of the funeral, no crying is permitted at the *sora* rite, which is celebrated on the sixth day after death, 'the day of rising'.[30] At graveside ceremonies or other funeral libations, the Sierra Leone Krio do not permit any tears, even from a wife or daughter. The clan must assume courage, and demonstrate by it that the enemy has not routed them.

This re-grouping of the family and sometimes the clan leads to a further factor in burial rites. Among the Mende, for example, before the body is laid to rest relatives and friends gather around and recount their grievances against the deceased. Creditors demand payment of his debts, and a relative stands surety for them even if only nominally. All those whom the deceased has offended grant him free forgiveness, so that the curse generated by human ill-will does not pursue him beyond the grave.[31] Other groups, for example the Yoruba and Akan, recount the activities of a deceased man, naming his faults and failures as well as his virtues.[32] The reasoning which dictates this ritual seems obvious. The West African lives primarily not as an individual but as a member of a group consisting of living and dead members. At death he is parted from the segment of the living. So the surviving relatives and friends seek to set out his life history in such a way that ultimately he leaves behind a happy memory. But he must not be left to wander aimlessly in the still unknown land of the dead. Moreover, the band of those who have predeceased him must be encouraged to give him a warm welcome as he joins the family again. The Mende and the Akan, for example, give him a present to take to the fathers as he crosses the river. In every case it is hoped that he will join them in *lannya-golehum* or *Dada-golehum*, the City of the White Sand (the Mende), or *Orun Emin*, the 'Good *Orun*', the 'White *Orun*' (the Yoruba: *Orun* means heaven), or *samandow* (the Akan).[33] The whole clan of living and dead must hold together in the life on earth as well as in the life after death. So at ancestral rites when the ancestors are mentioned by name, there is always added a blanket invocation of 'all you others whom we cannot now mention by name', to cover the recent dead who may have been omitted or the dead of long ago whose names none of the living members of the family or clan can recall. The Krio have an amusing custom by which, while the spokesman is calling out the names of the dead, others present at the ceremony freely interject additional names so the list is as complete as possible. When no other name is forthcoming, they then employ the blanket formula mentioned above.[34]

3.   DEATH AS TRANSFORMATION

Particularly among groups like the Akan of Ghana, the Yoruba, and the Temne, who hold a theory of divine kingship, death is also believed to be a transformation. The Akan king was supposed to hold court in the kingdom of *Nyankopon*, and to exercise jurisdiction over the spirits of his former subjects. Danquah, for example, states that the *opanyi* (i.e., chief) who had led an exemplary life was deified at death.[35] Besides, the soul of an Akan king had bestowed upon it the sum total of the divine-rulership of his predecessors. For the rank and file members of the community, the Akan would say that, when a man's life-soul (*kra*) is full of goodness, it ceases to be subject to reincarnation, and becomes a guardian spirit of the family.[36] The Yoruba hold a like notion of the *ori*, which essentially represents a man's destiny. At death, it ultimately becomes the guardian angel of the surviving members of the family.[37]

It is not easy to piece together into a simple statement the considerations which have led to some of the existing explanations of death. Suffice it to say that the death of an old person is accepted as a natural consequence of age. A man or woman who lives to a ripe old age goes through a manifest physical transformation, his powers fail, and life becomes a burden. The pregnant phrase 'second childhood' summarises how life comes full circle and virility yields to increasing infirmity. At death the transformation is complete. He now becomes spirit. As spirit the dead are nearer to God. So the Mende talk of those who died long ago as being in God's bosom. As a result of this proximity to God, they can now apprehend truth without being affected by personal prejudices. The Krio express this idea by referring to their dead ancestors as being in the world of truth (*tru wol*). The Yoruba appeal to them as impartial jurors to adjudicate between two contesting friends, while the Mende never do, so as not to induce them to take sides. In both cases, the ground of the attitude is the fact that the dead cannot but see the truth when an appeal is made to them.

4.   THE ORIGIN OF DEATH

Professor E.B. Idowu tells us that the Yoruba assume that death is the lot of a person of mature age. 'Death is meant for the aged and . . . given the right conditions, every person should live to a ripe old age'.[38] So the Yoruba pray 'that we may not die young: that we may not attain an old age of wretchedness'.[39] However, death is a personified power believed to be created by and under commission from *Olodumare* (i.e., God).

The Temne of Sierra Leone maintain that at first death did not exist. Man lived on earth for a given number of years until God sent his messenger for him and he returned to God. One arrogant and conceited man however refused to accompany the messenger. So a year later God sent two messengers, a young man called Sickness who weakened the rebel, followed by an old man, Death, who took him away.[40] The Mende, also of Sierra Leone, say that there was no death in the primal days, but God sent a dog to the world with a message, 'Life has come', and a toad saying, 'Death has come'. The two animals set off in a race. The dog, distracted by the smell of cooking, stopped at a house to eat while the toad went on. By the time the dog caught up with the toad, the people of the village had already been told, 'Death has come, Death has come!' The dog's proclamation of life was too late to be effective.[41] Other such stories abound all over West Africa. The obvious theme is that death is a contradiction of the hopes and aspirations of the living. The most virile man softens as he becomes ill and then dies. The baby with all the promise of life dies, and the promise is cut short, unfulfilled. Parents, relatives, wives, and children have to review the pattern of their life when the vigorous bread-winner dies and leaves a whole line of dependents unprovided for. At the same time, there lies implicit in the Temne and Mende myths the suggestion that death is the result of disobedience to God's will. In the one case, man's arrogance brings it about, and in the other, the dog's distraction from the race with the toad. In the one case, the man preferred not to leave the wealth he had acquired; in the other, the dog took time off to eat a bone.

5. THE DEATH OF GOD

At the same time, there is a strand of thinking which seeks to suggest that death stands over against God; indeed, it seems that God too was believed to be subject to death. However, this thought is rejected, perhaps because man revolts at the outcome of his thinking. We give two examples.

(a) The Akan have a saying that *Odamankoma*, the third name in their triadic deity, 'created death, but death killed him'. This difficult saying is countered by another which states that 'it was none but *Odamankoma* who made Death eat poison'[42]; that is to say, *Odamankoma* destroyed death. Danquah interprets the first statement to mean that *Odamankoma* represents 'the totality of both being and non-being', and that 'the mystery of life does not end in death but in life, the life that supersedes the death'. He seems to be regarded as embodying in himself both life and death. It is possible that the notion of the death of *Odamankoma* derives from the daily circuit of the sun as it rises in the east and sets in the west to rise again the next day. In an agricultural community, the diurnal motions of the sun are symbolic of life and death. But plants seem to continue to grow during the night in spite of the lack of sunlight. Has this contradiction affected Akan thinking about God?

(b) The Yoruba are more subtle in stating this point. *Olodumare* is not said to have died. He is said to have visited a priest and offered a sacrifice, including a large piece of white cloth with which he later covered himself as a protection from death. He thus remained eternal and is envisaged as a hoary old man.[43]

It is not easy to fathom the implications of these two examples. But one can reasonably conclude that a dualism is implicit in both myths, in spite of the explicit suggestion that God created all the spirit-influences in the world, as well as all the natural objects ranging from man to trees and rocks.

6.   CONCLUSION

Death, it can be said, is regarded by the tribes of West Africa which have been mentioned as man's great enemy. Perhaps, apart from God, it is of all spiritual agencies the most dreaded. It seems capable of making it impossible for man to fulfil the destiny given him by God at birth. It frustrates man's well-laid plans and changes the future life of dependents of its victims. But death is thought of in another dimension also. The personality of man is not dissolved by death. Indeed, death seems to be regarded as a kind of catalyst which makes man's personality blossom to its fullest – whether for good or for evil. So the good man at his death continues to be good without the ethical distortions associated with moral evil. The wicked man can become evil without any redeeming spark of goodness to brighten up his character.

For those groups which postulate divine kingship, death is certainly a road to deification. There seems to be a widespread belief that the deceased ancestors, ruler and subjects alike, live close to God, thus possessing both omniscience and a full grasp of truth. At the same time, death is a cheat. It cheats babies and young people of the full span of life, depriving them of the good things of nature. It also cheats the family and the clan of love and service from the beloved. But the clan or family must not seem to be defeated by death; so funeral rites are performed to restore its confidence whenever one member dies. At the same time, the unity of the living with the dead members of a family or clan is ensured by messages or presents from the living sent through a deceased member to the larger section of the family on the other side. But this reunion is not automatic. Every deceased person faces a bar of judgement. Here difficulties arise. Wicked persons, if they can be identified as witches, are condemned immediately, and are given no chance to survive. The contradiction which results from the disaster of the termination of life on the one hand, and the hope of a continuation of the same life on the other, perhaps explains the postulation of the soul, or, as in the case of the Akan, two souls. So death occurs when the soul departs from the body. But what is the source of the soul? The answer to this question varies with different tribes. One common answer is, 'It comes from God'. So at death it goes back to God. How then can a clan soul-commune be postulated? For this the Akan postulate two souls, the one a spark of God (*Nyame*), the other an extension of the father. Other groups like the Mende and the Yoruba seem to postulate only one soul which comes from God and goes back to God, but also joins the family spirit-commune which is in close regular touch with the living. In every case the spirits or souls of the dead are pure. This purity is taken for granted by the Akan, but sometimes, as among the Mende, gestures of spontaneous and voluntary forgiveness are offered to the dead so their souls can depart unencumbered by the sense of guilt which their unwitting actions may have caused. High-handed sins, usually described as witchcraft, are however not forgivable, except, as among the Akan, by the king. This attitude to witches, who ordinarily are believed to cause the death of children, to make men impotent and women barren, may suggest that a witch is seen as an incarnation of death or the principle of death. So while the burial rites for one approved by society are designed, through the inclusion of dances, to reassure the clan that they are not routed by death, the great enemy, the wicked are dismembered or burned. They remain unmourned.

PSYCHE IN CONFLICT[1]

An Enquiry into some Aspects of Psychic Influence in the African Understanding of Life

1. THE POSTULATE OF MULTIPLE SOULS IN MAN

Many African peoples believe that man has multiple souls. The Akan postulate two, the *kra*, the life-soul and the *sunsum* or *ntoro*, or personality soul; the Yoruba, according to Bascomb name three: the ancestral guardian soul (*ɛlɛda, ipɔnri*) associated with the head and re-incarnation; the breath (*ɛmí*) which resides in the lungs and chest; the shadow (*ojiji*) which seems merely to follow the living body about, and has no function.[2] Idowu and Lucas however also accept a multiciplicity of souls among the Yoruba but set out a different pattern. The Ibo also maintain there are four souls. P. Amaury Talbot sets them out as follows: first, an ethereal soul, the double and inner frame of the physical form; secondly, the soul prayer, the consciousness, the thinking or mental body; third, the spiritual or minor Ego; and fourth, the Over-Soul or *Chi*, the great Spirit, which often includes several lesser Egos and always 'stays with God'.[3] Like the Ibo, the Nupe also refer to four souls. On the other hand, the Mende of Sierra Leone, seem to postulate only one, the *ngafa*, which is also spirit, but which is supposed to be able to leave the body when a person is asleep.[4] Witches operate through it at night. These concepts of the spirit-consistency of man should be related to the notion that man is made up of flesh and blood, on the one hand, and spirit matter, on the other. While accepting the physical element of human nature, there also seems to be a widespread belief that man is 'divine' in origin. The Akan *kra* is a spark of divinity coming from Nyame, the Lunar Mother-Goddess, and enters into the bloodstream of a pregnant mother at a ceremony when, according to Antubam, a few minutes before birth, the child is washed in 'water of purity and sanctity' by its tutelar sponsor. God utters a brief message of life, *nkrabea*, 'into the mouth of the child from an *Adwera*

67

leaf in his hand' presumably using a drop of water. This drop of life water penetrates the whole body of the child, wakes it up 'to life' and, later, becoming *Ikera* (kra), (a spiritual likeness of God), settles down in the child as its life-long spiritual guide and life giver. So 'man is born sacred and free of sin' or 'he is sacred and pure at birth',[5] Danquah supports this view by saying that the Akan 'is born the purest soul with an *nkrabea* ordained and endowed for him direct from and by the hands of Nyankopon'.[6] The Yoruba trace the *ɛmí(n)* to Olorun, the Supreme Deity, and therefore regard it as 'the divine element in him' (man).[7]

The Ibo Over-Soul, the *Chi*, is of the same *timbre* since the Supreme Being is *CHI*. Talbot observes that 'Few people believe in all four souls in the sense that they possess distinct names for each, and some combine the mental and spiritual bodies into one conception, while the existence of the Over-Soul is not clearly appreciated by all; but the greater number postulate in essence the existence of the four souls, which are instruments through which the Ego is able to function in the various planes'.[8] At the same time, he observes:

'the physical frame is the most material and furthest removed from the spiritual; no negro ever identifies himself with it or with the ethereal body. Both are purely physical and temporary. The personality of an individual is contained in the soul and spirit, but the real Ego exists essentially in the Over-Soul, which, with the Spirit, is more in touch with God and is not deeply influenced by events affecting its various emanations comprised in the physical, ethereal and mental forms and the shadow'.[9]

So too the Mende believe that the *ngafa* comes from God and enters the mother's body like the *kra*, thus inspiring and giving life to her blood, that is to the foetus.

2. MAN: DIVINE AND PROFANE

How then does this divine element in man manifest itself? Let us first consider the Ghanaian situation which seems easy to discuss. Antubam suggests that the *kra* (*okera*) is supposed to be the 'spiritual root force' of a man's conscience and influences all his actions. He goes on to say that 'there is a belief that one's *Okera* (*kra*) is in action, whenever one gives a sincere and honest judgment; for it helps the mind to see between good and evil . . . Whether or not one be

68

good-natured is also determined by the active existence of an *Okera* in one'.[10] Christaller did suggest that 'the *kra* is considered partly as a separate being, distinct from the person, who protects him, . . . gives him good or bad advice, causes his undertakings to prosper or slights or neglects him . . . and therefore in the case of prosperity receives thanks and thank-offerings like a fetish'.[11] Williamson, on the other hand, questions the validity of this notion and suggests that it is difficult to accept that the *kra* could give bad advice, but admits that many think that the promptings of the *kra* are always good and to obey them 'endangers one's peace of mind'. He however concedes that it is probable that the *kra* may slight or neglect a man 'when he has done something to offend it'.[12] One would then infer any inactivity of the *kra* constitutes neglect which leads to a condition that may result in sickness, calamity, distress or death; otherwise, the *kra* would defend and protect its owner from harm and danger.[13] Margaret Field however mentions the notion of a 'bad kla' (*kra*) present among the Ga and adds, 'one of the commonest causes of sickness . . . is an annoyed *kla*'.[14] Meyerowitz also presents a related picture of the *kra* when she says that the concept, after undergoing several stages of evolution, became 'the source of man's good and bad fortune' after it was no longer envisaged as a life-force only 'animating an inert body, but had come to represent the impersonal and divine soul in god and man.'[15] There is thus a dual relation of identity and separateness between the *kra* and the individual. 'A bad conscience and ill-will towards others are said to disturb the peace of the indwelling spirit (*kra*) which in turn disturbs the owner's health'.[16] We recall Debrunner's comment that 'in sickness the *kra* is sometimes supposed to be seen behind a person as a separate being', 'a sort of double, having legs, arms, head, heart etc., like the material body, only of a finer substance'.[17]

But the *kra* needs the medium of the *sunsum* to manifest itself in practical life. So Danquah refers to the *sunsum* as 'the bearer of conscious experience, that is to say, the experiential aspect of man who is subject to the environment'[18]; it provides the medium in which the *kra* grows and affords it an expression of the advice mentioned in an earlier paragraph. In modern times, the *sunsum* has been identified with the *ntoro* which is more related to the notion that the father of the child is the 'natural custodian of life-stream, sanctity, and the power of procreation'. Antubam goes on to state that the *ntoro* 'seeks to provide and sustain three essential spiritual properties of life in the individual society'.[19] First, 'it seeks to provide and maintain purity in the individual'; second, it gives 'strength, activity and singleness of character in the individual'; third, it provides 'the individual awareness of spiritual powers and the wisdom to acquire and maintain them'[20] for his benefit.

As far back as 1777, Oldendorp, a Moravian missionary, had observed that the Ga priests understand diseases as the result of a 'misunderstanding between spirit and soul (personality-soul and life-soul)'. In their opinion as long as the two live together in peace and concord like husband and wife, man is healthy, but if one of the two commits a fault, the harmony is disturbed: the pure part wants to separate itself from the impure one, hence arise inner trouble and sickness of the body. The priest, as physician, therefore challenges the conscience of the patient to get to know the sins which have attracted his illness. If these are fully confessed, the priest begins the treatment. At first, the root of the illness is removed by offering sacrifice to the impure part and by pronouncing or fulfilling vows; thus the concord between spirits and soul is re-established.'[21]

It is therefore significant that the Akan also believe that a person's *sunsum* 'may get hurt or knocked about or become sick, and so make the body ill.' Rattray quotes an Ashanti informant as saying, 'Very often, although there may be other causes, e.g. witchcraft, ill-health is caused by the evil and hate that another has in his head against you (someone). Again you too may have hatred in your head against another, because of something that person has done to you, and that too causes your *sunsum* to fret and become sick. Our forebears knew this to be the case, and so they ordain a time, once every year, when every man and woman, free man and slave, should have freedom to speak out just what was in their head to tell their neighbours just what they thought of them, and of their actions, and not only their neighbours, but also the king and chief. When a man has spoken thus he will feel his *sunsum* cool and quieted, and the *sunsum* of the other person against whom he has spoken will be quieted too.'[22] The Yoruba *okebadan*, held annually in Ibadan affords the same emotional outlet to the inhabitants of that city.[23] The relationship between the *Kra* and the *sunsum* as contributory to health and well-being is seen in that witches use the *sunsum* for their nocturnal activities but they are said to attack the *kra* of their victim.[24]

The Yoruba concept of the divine in man seems more complex, but may be set out as follows using J.O. Lucas and E.B. Idowu as our guide. Lucas postulates:

(i) a heart-soul (*ɔkan*) which can go out of the body and appear in dreams, leaves the body at the death but may be re-incarnated. Witches use *ɔkan* which metamorphoses into a bird.

(ii) a spiritual soul (*ɛmí*), the seat of life and therefore the 'divine element' in man. The *ɛmí* depends on the heart-soul for its

70

self-realisation. One is reminded of the Akan *kra* and *sunsum*, the ɛmí being analogical to the *kra* and ɔkan to *sunsum*. For Lucas *ipɔri* means a man's destiny.[25]

Idowu admits ɛmí is an 'invisible and intangible' element of man, equivalent to spirit. It is that which 'breathes in man', although it is also used for 'life' as the bare fact of animate existence.[26] He observes that 'the breath is not ɛmí but ēmi, adding in a footnote that 'ɛmí can assume a visible, tangible form as when it comes out of the witch, takes wings and flies like a bird!' It may also be seen 'as an apparition'. ɔkan, for Idowu, is, simply, heart and 'is the seat of the emotion and psychic energy'. He then goes on to say, 'the soul, to the Yoruba, is the "inner person" which he terms *ori*, – the personality-soul. The physical head, ori is therefore a symbol of the *ori-inu* – the internal head – 'that rules, controls and guides the "life" and activities of the person.'[27] So the *Ori* has an experiential aspect. At the same time, according to Idowu, 'Ori derives directly from *Olodumare* and therefore like the *kra* of the Akan, it holds a man's destiny'.[28] In addition, *Ori* is also conceived as a 'semi-split' entity, ɛnikeji, a man's double, his 'guardian angel' and 'protector' – 'the essence of a man's individual personality which must be kept in harmony ('on good terms') with him. As such, sacrifices ought to be offered to it, in respect of this semi-split entity.[29] One such sacrifice consists of 'kola-nuts, fish, fowl or an animal victim which are offered, a piece of the kola-nut or fish stuck on the forehead, while the blood of the fowl or animal is smeared on it'.[30] This is a cleansing ceremony no doubt.

Idowu is in effect saying that the *ori-inu* is the energic element in man which is symbolised by the visible *ori* – one's natural head.

J.O. Lucas disagrees sharply with Idowu's interpretation of *Ori* as expressive of the personality-soul. For him, *Ori* is the visible head although 'among some tribes, a spirit is supposed to dwell in the head (physical head) and is worshipped periodically with a view to securing good luck'. But he continues, 'Never, is *Ori* regarded in Yorubaland as the essence of personality, or the personality-soul' Lucas admits that *ipa* combined with *ori*, thus becoming *ipɔri*, 'Is regarded as indicating a man's destiny.'[31]

The discussion on *ori* and *ori-inu* has been taken a stage further by the Rev. E.A. Adegbola.[32] Adegbola refers to two major uses of the term *ori*, the first representing the person of the individual, and a second in respect of an *invisible* (inner) entity, *ori-inu*.

Ori, per se, is prominent in a cult of the head, *ipɔnri* which prescribes sacrifices to be offered to the head – 'personalised and therefore fit to be propitiated, cajoled or soothed.'[33] It can imply

71

one's lot or predestination. But the *head* is also 'the avenger spirit, "catching" those who have wronged the owner of the head.' Adegbola goes on to state, that, depending on the context, 'the head' may be interpreted to mean the mode of creation of man, his natural tendencies, lot or predestination, or the hereditary factor which constitutes ancestor worship. We are face to face, first, with forces over which a man has no control, and, second, with the will and personal character of the individual concerned. It is therefore imperative that a man 'hears' the dictates of his head, whether in respect of food taboos or the vocation he should follow (odu). *Ori-inu*, on the other hand, is an invisible (inner) entity which according to Adegbola is generally identified with character; the character of the individual. He agrees with Idowu that it is essential that a harmonious relation be maintained between the external head and the internal head for a successful career in life. Thus a person who stands the chance of success or good fortune – a mark of his external head – may encounter failure if his internal head is bad, i.e. 'if he is unsociable, irascible, proud, disrespectful, ruthless, greedy of gain'; his 'internal head' has corrupted his 'external head'.[34] The Yoruba therefore cater for this contingency by using suggestion and 'religious moralisations'. A cultic rite involving the washing of the individual's shaven head with water freshly drawn from the river early in the morning, into which some herbs are rubbed and into which 'the Ifa powder on which has been inscribed the Odu (oracle) that refers to a good head' may have been blown, is prescribed by a diviner to reform his, the suppliant's, character and so provide a restorative of the destined success of the individual by integrating his character with his destiny (Odu). The patient meanwhile beats his head, and confesses his past faults. After praying to do better, he is then admonished by the priest to observe 'particular moral taboos in the name of the gods'. In other words, the internal head is experiential.[35]

Adegbola's interest in the essay to which we have been referring is ethical, so he does not go on to introduce a discussion of illness and his interpretation of the Yoruba understanding of the causes thereof. But in view of the fact that when a child is born an *Ifa* priest sets out a number of taboos which he must observe and keep, we may cross the line and suggest that violation of such taboos would militate against the well-being of the individual concerned. As another author, Swailem Sidhom, in the same collection of essays, observes:

'Sickness . . . is not normal, therefore it is a threat to man's security. The possible causes are, then, to be found. Is it the wages of disobedience, disrespect, or of ignorant (we would add,

72

deliberate) breaking of the tabus? Could, it be a greedy ancestor or a malicious enemy that moved something from outside (such as a foreign substance or an evil spirit) to enter into the body of the sick person?'[36] Adegbola's 'unsociable, irascible, proud, disrespectful, ruthless, greedy of gain'[37] fits into Sidhom's catalogue. Such an individual may disrespect a farmer's claim to his crops even when a protective charm guards it; or he may neglect his ancestors; or he may violate one or more of his personal taboos, thus demonstrating the tendencies attributed to the 'internal head'. The consequence is illness, sometimes leading to death. Thinking about such illness rationally, we would attribute it to psycho-somatic causes. But in primitive African thinking the conflict which exists in the individual's subconscious is personalised and attributed to an external cause which is also personalised, acting in a manner, as in this case, against the internal head, itself personalised.

The Mende of Sierra Leone, as has been noted, do not seem to have more than one soul, i.e the *ŋgafa* which comes from God and is of divine origin. But they also hold that each *ŋgafa* comes to the world impregnated with the destiny of the individual, *nɛmi*, which is described as a tiny embryonic shrub with a potential for growth. Every individual must therefore take care to nurse his *nɛmi* by so behaving to others, in particular his elders, that they utter a word of blessing on him, from time to time. This blessing would be invoked by his good behaviour and willingness to accept the guidance of those older than himself – in short, by the nature of his character. Whenever such a blessing is uttered, the Mende believe that the destiny shrub receives a watering, *hɛɛ-niɛì*, 'prayer showers'.[38] The more sociable the individual is, the bigger the shrub becomes. On the contrary, the less amenable the individual is to the elementary demands of his society, the greater the risk of the shrub withering and ultimately dying. This latter condition, it is believed, prevails when a person is cursed by another, and in particular, by his mother and mother's brother. He then suffers from misfortune of various intensities which in a severe form may lead to mental strain and consequently illness.[39] The Mende situation seems to reflect the Akan and Yoruba attitudes we have considered earlier.

3. PSYCHOLOGICAL ILLNESSES AND MISFORTUNE: MAGIC OR CONFLICT?

It is in this context that we wish briefly to raise questions related to the attitude of most African peoples to sickness, restricting the

73

discussion to what we would call psychological cases. As it is well known, there are two layers of treatment for illnesses, the one physical, and the other psychological. Lists exist of curatives for physical illnesses which investigators like Northcote Thomas, Karl Leman, George W. Harley, Margaret Field and Michael Gelfand, among others, have collected from Sierra Leone, the Kongo, Liberia, Ghana and Mashonaland.[40] The Yoruba curatives are also well-known. At the same time one finds, for example, the widespread belief that a husband will have swollen legs or some other ailment, if his wife holds sexual congress with another man; he may be killed in battle or miss his victim at a hunt; he may be unsuccessful in a business enterprise which takes him away from home. Again the curse of a woman who feels she had been badly treated by a man with whom she had been intimate may destroy him. The curse of an elder, more so of a parent, is believed to have adverse effects on the offending individual.

The Nyakyusa, indeed, believe that a newly married bride must not meet her parents, especially her mother, on the day following the consummation of the marriage without going through a specified ritual by which the husband becomes identified with them. Failing that the mother will suffer from diarrhoea.[41] The Bemba mother has to keep on putting out fires at her hearth in case she had been visited by someone who had been involved in recent sex-acts, otherwise her child would die.[42] The Ibo believe that if a woman who has committed adultery prepares food for her husband the Earth-Goddess, Ala, will 'catch her and she and her children will die.'[43] At Nri, in Iboland, no woman may have sexual intercourse even with her husband while preparing food. She must wait till the food is cooked and ready for serving.[44]

Among the Thonga, it is forbidden for a woman in pregnancy to visit a sick person or else the latter might die.[45] Groups like the Yoruba, the Mende and the Lele, for example, hold the view that brawls and other forms of anger and ill-will between persons militate against the well-being of a community. The Lovedu believe that the unexpressed anger of one's father's sister may cause the son to be ill. Margaret Field sets out the situation neatly when she observes that 'anger, bitterness, and resentment against others, especially if allowed to rankle secretly without finding speech, are commonly recognised causes of illness' among the Ga of Ghana.[46] In the same vein, the Nyakyusa stress what is usually termed 'the breath of men' meaning, first, the unexpressed anger which may cause illness; thus a father's anger may cause his married daughter to be sterile, if he disapproves of the husband. But, *per contra*, the uttered forgiveness overcomes misfortunes and illness when an offender pleads for forgiveness by the person offended, especially so if the offended party is a senior member of the community.[47] Indeed, Fadipe calls attention to the fact that among the Yoruba, a curse pronounced by an elder person against a younger offender is efficacious.[48] Among the Sierra Leone Creole and the Mende for example, a mother's curse is greatly feared. Middleton writing of the Lugbara referring to cases of old women who had been struck by their sons comments that this is 'a terrible offence'.[49]

The potency of nudity when practised by women whether among the Ba-Nkumba of South Africa or the Creole of Sierra Leone or by men as in the case of the Azande father who takes his penis in his hand, blows upon it and curses his son, or other cases of an older person cursing a younger offending person, all lead to psychic conditions which have adverse effects on the object of the curse employed.[50] We could cite a multiplicity of these cases. After careful study, we are constrained to say that among African peoples, there is a widespread belief that misfortune and illness are closely linked together and derive from hostile external personalised forces. The situation is complicated by the use of charms and like objects usually referred to, among writers both African and from the West, as magic. Someone may, for example, set up a stub of firewood, fixed on to a short stick or maybe a pole, in his vegetable garden or cassava farm and utter an invocation which includes words to the effect that anyone other than the owner of the garden or farm who removes any of the crops would suffer from violent stomach pains; if an empty tortoise-shell is used, the victim should suffer simultaneously from vomiting and diarrhoea – associated magic, they say. One finds, however that a thief naturally falls ill suffering from the anticipated illness and has to confess his crime in good time to be relieved of the curse of the invocation or else he might die.[51] There is the interesting situation where, as among the Limba of Sierra Leone, the protective *medicine*, it is believed, kills the *guilty* person and may go on 'to destroy in turn his whole family;' however, it does not attack one who participates of the booty if he had been unaware of the theft.[52] The Mende, again of Sierra Leone, always add a venial clause when they set a medicine in a cassava farm, which infers no theft, when a man who is on a long journey comes across a farm, and feeling hungry takes up a root, eats enough to satiate his hunger and leaves the rest behind. He never falls ill.[53] The ill-effects of the curse laid on the farm (and the immunity where this is applicable) or, for that matter, the misfortune that follows mother's curse, is no doubt attributable to a *sensus communis*, based on the instruction on good

75

behaviour and honesty which each member of the community would have received in childhood. But is there also in each community, in addition to the *sensus communis*, a contributory psychic factor homologous to a collective *kra*, which is related to the *sensus communis* as a collective *sunsum* of a given community – that is to say a collective sub-consciousness backed by an equally vital collective consciousness.[54] It is significant that among the Mende of Sierra Leone when a curse is laid in respect of, say, stolen property, all who were accessories both before and after the act, all who could be presumed to be accessories – father, mother, wife – are all included in the directives issued when the curse is laid. Or again, when a Mende mother's brother curses a nephew all the brothers and sisters must join the offending nephew when the curse is revoked.[55] Indeed, there is a general feeling among the Mende that not only does a curse spread its effects laterally among potential culprits, but it also works its way down vertically, with serious effects on younger members of a family or group. Are we now approaching the area of magic in its wider from? We would here observe that the concept of the magical, however true it may appear to be in some cases, does not altogether provide a satisfactory answer in respect of the cases we have been discussing. It is a matter of some surprise that Dr. J.O. Lucas, a man of considerable perspective, allowed himself to describe taboos as 'negative magic' whilst 'the forms of sorcery, exercise of mysterious powers for good or ill, use of charms and the practice of occultism for therapeutic or other purposes, and performances based on a claim to possession or esoteric and mysterious knowledge rank as positive magic'.[56] The application of the term to all the situations in Dr. Lucas' classification in the way it is stated creates problems. If, as Lucas rightly suggests, 'Africans desire "life, health and strength" not only in this world but also in the next: . . . '[57] then do they understand some of the situations which we call magical differently from us? Let us take the case of the curse which a Lovedu's father's sister could bring upon a nephew or niece by merely nursing a grievance which she does not utter. According to J.D. and E.J. Krige, the force unleashed, known as *mahava*, may cause illness in the family of her brother's home. The Kriges explain that this is not witchcraft but merely 'concealed complaints, repressed and subconscious wants' which create a tension in the minds of one's near relatives. They also add that 'the dissatisfaction in a (Lovedu) mother's heart, whether conscious or unconscious, in connexion with her daughter's marriage may cause her sterility'.[58]

It is interesting to note that the ill effects of the *mahava* seem to demand the intervention of the ancestors for the removal of the

76

illness caused. Again, Fr. Jarrett-Kerr reports the use of a painting of Jesus Christ as an ancestor in an African mission hospital in South Africa to which was attributed the success of the hospital. In another hospital, which was run by the Government, as it was not possible to use a picture of Jesus, the doctor hung up on the wall above the table in his consulting room a picture of two Swazi chiefs. So whenever he found a consultant needed hospitalisation he looked up at the Swazi and then said to the patient: 'Yes, they tell me you should come into hospital'. And this dictum of the ancestral chiefs worked[59] – to hospital the patient came.

There also exist records of cases of physical illnesses which could not be readily relieved by ordinary scientific medical treatment but which have been cured after certain propitiatory and expiatory rites have been performed. Herbal curatives are also employed but it seems to us that the cures are attributed to the propitiatory– expiatory rites, even though Monica Wilson takes the opposite view.[60]

Harris and Sawyerr report the case of a man who had been in a mission hospital in the provinces of Sierra Leone on a diagnosis of advanced pulmonary pneumonia and presumably looked near hopeless. He was however removed from hospital by his relatives, taken overnight over a long journey to the grave of a deceased brother whose funeral rites he had somehow neglected. Special propitiatory rites were performed and the man was reported to have been seen walking about in the town in which he lived a few days afterwards, apparently whole and well.[61] Harley has a large number of such cases recorded for us.[62] Lucas' comment that in the West African's desire for 'life, health and strength', 'prayers and offerings are made for the dead, and everything possible is done to secure their welfare'[63] in the context of magic is significant. Harris and Sawyerr have recorded a form of words used when a *medicine* was set on a kola-tree to protect it from marauders which, translated into English from Mende, reads – 'O ŋgewɔ, God, You medicine, which I am hanging on this kola-tree, see that you hold (fast) anyone, who comes to steal of its fruit. Under the protection, or by the power of my father's spirit'.[64] The association of the ancestral spirit is significant, with ŋgewɔ in the background. We recall Trowell's comment that 'the African child is reared in a world where ghosts are more real than men, a world in the control of spirits of the dead'. He adds, 'Magical conceptions and magical causations are the only facts of his philosophy. The pleasure or anger of the spirits are the cause of all disease, famine, death, and the whole range of natural science'.[65] It is possible to attribute the belief that a patient will recover if the ancestors are placated during

77

an illness, to mythical thinking, a belief which persists even among African University students, particularly so in cases of anxiety neurosis. Thus a Nigerian undergraduate student studying in Sierra Leone comes to feel that his uncle whose children had not done well at school would be envious of his father and, of course, of him; somehow, he breaks down under this anxiety and has to attend the clinic at a mental hospital. He had developed a guilt-complex not understood by anyone with a modern scientific training.

We may well ask, is his illness due to magic or, as has been suggested, to a guilt-complex generated by a situation over which he has no control?

4. THE PROBLEM OF GUILT AMONG AFRICANS

That term, guilt, raises a number of questions. We are reminded of names like J.V. Taylor, Fred Welbourn and Meyer Fortes who stress that the African belongs to a shame-and not to a guilt-culture. Fortes is quite categorical about the Tallensi belonging to a shame-culture.[66] Welbourn following Erickson, describes guilt as the experience a child has when he fails to use the autonomy of his individual existence 'to display *initiative*'.[67] Shame, on the other hand, is 'an emotional response to falling short of a social norm'. But it might not be felt 'unless the actions became known to others'.[68] At the same time, guilt-feelings, are based on factors which are 'under no conscious control'. They may be caused by the disapproval of others, even if the agent believes himself morally right. They may be a response to simple ill-will towards others, or to choice between incompatible loyalties. They may rise from the deep unconscious with no known object'. This distinction is difficult to maintain, whatever the community may be. Shame is 'tradition directed' response whilst guilt is 'inner-directed'. Welbourn however, concedes that 'members of traditional societies are able to project on to mystical beings much that inner-directed men, whose guilt-feelings are much nearer the surface, must take upon their own shoulders'.[70] But this projection of one's behaviour is not peculiar to African traditional Society. Much of the Christian teaching on Satan leads towards this defect.

We would say that guilt and shame are often seen appearing together as sometimes happens when a thief is caught. He certainly feels guilty, when the owner of the stolen object comes upon him; but he is also ashamed maybe for having been caught. Happily, Monica Wilson and others do not make this sharp distinction between tradition–directed and inner-directed Africans. Instead, they postulate sin and guilt of African peoples.[72] J.V. Taylor does not, however, exclude a 'sense of sin' among Africans; he postulates that 'it may be wandering about in disguise'.[73] So he goes on to say, 'The essence of sin in the primal view is that it is anti-social.[74]

We may have to decide whether the content of sin must always mean sin against God, or it could mean sin against our fellowmen although ultimately resolving itself into sin against God. Perhaps Christian systematic theologians would at some time seek to resolve this problem for the ordinary Christian man and woman. It however seems clear that in the African situation, the various taboos and other prohibitions established by protective *medicines* set up in farms or the dread of mother's curse, could be in some way or the other related to the violation of a law (*parabasis*) even if (as it is the case in many instances) such a law may not have been codified. In that case, it would be difficult to reject the suggestion that inner-directedness i.e. the force of the feeling of a sense of guilt can and does exist among many peoples. And if it does, then is it the source of that collective sub-consciousness which is manifest in the individuals who suffer specific ailments when they steal on a farm or increasingly lose a grip of themselves when they know their father or mother or some member of their community has cursed them? So we ask, if a Nykyusa girl of marriageable age runs away with a man of whom her father does not approve, does she develop a sense of fear of the father's anger, and accordingly a sense of guilt which disturbs her emotional equilibrium and makes it difficult for her to conceive a child, other things being equal? The answer seems to be in the affirmative. Such a situation is not peculiar to Africans as such. We would therefore invite Welbourn and others who hold like views to listen to Henry McKeating's observations: 'Guilt feelings . . . are inseparable from the nature of man. They arise out of the tension between his self-directed and his other directed propensities. Often they are useful. Sometimes they are an embarrassment . . .'[75]

Unaware of the existence of bacteria, African peoples tend to assume that an illness is usually due to a supernatural influence having entered into his system. So although they are familiar with the medical properties of various herbs they resort to psychological methods, and the divining healing doctor whose regalia, incantations and dances create the appropriate climate which we have hitherto described as suggestibility. Some diseases, it is believed, are caused by 'a spirit capable of hearing'.[76] and can resist a cure if the medicine is named within the hearing of the patient. In reverse, we can appreciate why exorcism is a vital ingredient of many cures. We recall

Levi-Strauss' remark that 'the notion of a super-native exists only for a humanity which attributes supernatural powers to itself and in return ascribes the powers of its super-humanity to Nature'.[77]

5. THE DIVINITY IN MANY A CENSOR

Small wonder therefore that the African healing doctor attaches so much importance to 'confessions' whether of theft, adultery or anger. Patient and doctors alike believe in the confessional. Martin Jarrett-Kerr reports the case of a woman patient in a South African hospital who was suffering from a cardiac condition 'propped up in bed, with an oxygen mask on, struggling, restless', asking to see him in hospital. 'She wanted to see me. It wasn't only the panting for breath that made her restless: it was still more the knowledge that she might die and carry away with her a gangrenous secret which she wanted to have amputated . . . she wanted a "hamartectomy". In other words, she wanted to make her confession. Shriven, she slept that night – without oxygen.' Next morning, she received Holy Communion. Her progress continued and she was discharged from hospital a fortnight later.[78]

This confessional is not always held secret by African healing doctors because often the patients are accompanied by their relatives and friends. If the shrine is set in an open place, other members of the community who would have been attracted by the presence of the priest and his patient or patients may also hear the confession or confessions when they are made. We are therefore inclined to take the view that the *sensus communis* operates through the members of the community in a way comparable to the function or functions of the Akan *sunsum*. On the one hand, the listening audience become satisfied that the patient will, in the future, seek to live a life of spiritual purity consonant with the well-being of the community; and, on the other, the patient is given an opportuniy of recovering the good-will of the community when having been expurgated of his sin, he receives an implied promise of communal support for his future observance of the demands of the community. Even in cases of witchcraft, a person who had confessed to being a witch is often cured of the witch tendencies and restored to the general life of the community. As Adegbola mentions in the case of the *cult* of the head, at the end of the rite, the priest-healer admonishes the patient to observe certain accepted modes of conduct.[79] The offending person is regarded as having placed himself outside the pale of his community and is accordingly ostracized, albeit temporarily.

Everybody is angry with him. But when he confesses his fault, the anger of the community is stayed and he is restored once more to the family circle.[80] A few random instances will illustrate the last point: An Ibo or Lele husband would not allow his wife to cook his food if she is having her menses; nor would a Temne man unless he has only one wife.[81] A Lele woman believes that if another woman indulges in sex-relations in her hut during her absence her child would die; but she must be aware of the event.[82] The Kongo believe that a man and a woman who hold sex-congress on the ground will suffer from *Beela kwa Nsi*. Their stomachs will become stout and big; they will inevitably die.[83] But when a Kongo husband who had sought protection for his wife against the young men of the town, by invoking the service of a *nganga* dies, his widow cannot establish a new marital union until she has gone with the same *nganga* accompanied by others to the river-side; the others will move away but she and the *nganga* will have sex-relations and then 'bathe in the water together'.[84] Since Kongo sex regulations demand that all sexual intercourse must be held lying down, such mating must take place on the ground. But nothing happens to them. Is it the fact of communal approval that explains why the widow and the *nganga* do not fall ill and die, whilst the fear of being found out make others develop *Beela Kwa Nsi* and ultimately die?[85]

Monica Wilson's comment that the genius of Nyakyusa religion is an awareness of the corrupting power of 'anger in the heart' and of the necessity of confession and reconciliation if men are to be healthy in mind and body, is most applicable to our present discussion.[86] Evans-Pritchard makes a similar comment when he says of the Nuer, that they believe that sickness is a manifestation of the moral or spiritual state of the sufferer.[87]

Monica Wilson indeed goes a stage further when she observes that the efficacy of herbal cures is destroyed by quarrels in the family which uses them.[88] Are we then approaching a manifestation of an inner state of mind which is responsible for the onset of cases of psycho-somatic diseases, and which must be counteracted if a patient is to be cured of such illness? A medical friend once told the writer that Africans are not really afraid of death as Europeans are prone to be; indeed they seem to be resigned to the event. But they do not easily submit to situations which create social tensions. This is best exemplified by the principle which underlies the Nyakyusa 'breath of men' notion, a notion widely accepted among many African groups. Such groups accept that the correlative 'cool heart' comes when, on the one hand, the offending person acknowledges his offence and, on the other, the offended party equally admits a grievance. It seems therefore that the 'cool heart' provides the necessary ingredient for establishing *rapport* with a psychologically sick patient. The following instance will illustrate the point. The Akan explain delayed childbirth in terms of a protest made by the foetus, *mmota*, which is supposed to have the power of discerning that the mother had wronged the father by engaging in adulterous association with some other male.[89] This foetal principle of discernment, *mmota* – 'perception and judgment' – is identified with the blood of the father transmitted through the seminal fluid into the mother's body; it is believed to reside in her all through the period of gestation in symbiosis with her blood, as it happens in a blood-covenant relation.

As is well known, when the parties enter a blood-covenant by eating or drinking of each other's blood, it is assumed that the blood is not ingested as such when eaten or drunk by the other person. Instead, it remains unchanged and assumes a supervisory role, supporting the other member when the contract is fulfilled or destroying him when he is disloyal. We recall Evans-Pritchard's comments relating to the Azande that in a blood-covenant that the 'Azande say that the blood goes down into the stomach of a man and from there sees all that he does, and when a man betrays his blood-brother it avenges itself on him. The blood knows exactly what is required of the blood-brother because it has heard the address made to it when it was swallowed'.[90] The covenant always includes a form of words which lays down conditions which when fulfilled the parties will thrive; but if not, the offender will die.

Although marital relations to not imply the same form of words as the blood-covenant, yet the injunctions of parents to their daughters urging fidelity is homologous.

We now wish do suggest that the effect of cures often described in terms of the magical, and the correlative curses by equally magical methods, must be thought of in terms of the *mmota* principle which, residing in the individual, protests against his Ego-aspect. When this protest is made, the individual develops a low psychological tone which makes him ill. When therefore, as in the case of the Akan mother in childbirth, a confession is made of the sin committed, the struggle ceases and the patient is poised for recovery. The restored psychological tone of his mind makes his body responsive to the healing powers of herbal curatives.

6. CONCLUSION

Many African groups believe that man is innately divine, bearing either a spark of the divine fire (Akan) or holding within himself the divine breath (Yoruba, Mende). But this divine aspect, being invisible, needs a medium through which it may manifest itself. This medium is also of spirit-form but different in origin; it expresses itself through man's physical senses. The former is thus ethereal and the latter experiential in their respective modes of manifestation. The experiental aspect of man therefore comes under the influence of the environment whilst the divine aspect is believed to have a set line of development determined by the destiny it had received from God before the individual was born.

Again, the divine element of man is thought to be pure and not subject to corruption although the experiental aspect is readily liable to be. The well-being of the individual is therefore dependent on a harmonious relation between the two component factors of his make-up. Otherwise, the pure part seeks to separate itself from the impure and the individual becomes physically disturbed and may fall ill or even die. We therefore suggest that the effect of curses on man, within the African context, is not due to magic but to a conflict which is psychological in nature, created by the fear of a sin committed against the *sensus communis* of a given community and which gnaws into the psychic life of the offender, thereby causing him to be ill. As a result even when physical curatives are known which may be used to relieve the illness, experience has taught the African to first employ propitiatory-expiatory rites which offer the patient the spiritual cleansing which restores harmony between the Ego and the Id elements of his person and thus creates the condition which makes his body responsive to herbal curatives. Only when a patient responds to herbal curatives within the first three or four days is this procedure not adopted.

To achieve this end, most African healing doctors have not only devised attractive regalia but they also adopt psychological methods which include suggestion, the use of drums and dances accompanied by a form of words which convince the patient of his unworthiness. He is therefore more ready to confess his sins in the hope that the confession would afford him a psychological release, generally described as a 'cool heart'. At the same time, confession is also expected from any one who has been offended this time, by his open admission of his feeling of grievance.

So confession of guilt by the offender, backed by an admission of grievance by the offended party is followed by a ritual of purification which ranges from the offended party taking water in the mouth which he sprays on the head of the culprit, to a ritual bath, especially so, when a cultic spirit has been violated.

If this argument is accepted, then it seems that the too easy acceptance of the idea that these cures have a magical content should not be encouraged. We would prefer to say that the cures are psychological in nature.

This discussion has naturally been limited to illnesses which derive from curses which have created psychological factors; it does not cover either straightforward physical ailments or cases which have been attributed to witchcraft. It may yet be true that the term magic could be rightly applied to many other acts.

WHAT IS AFRICAN THEOLOGY?

1.   THE PROBLEM STATED

'The opportunity for evangelism has never been greater than it is now in Africa; but it will take a Church which is alive and vigorous with the power which only God can supply to be equal to the task'. So ends the final essay, written by Professor Bolaji Idowu of Ibadan, in a series of essays, representing Papers read at the Seventh International African Seminar, held in the University of Ghana in April, 1965.[1]

Idowu believes that the Church in Africa and Nigeria in particular had come into being 'with prefabricated theology, liturgies, and traditions'[2] and now bears little, if any, real relation to the indigenous beliefs and practices of the people to which it was brought. So on the one hand, Idowu acknowledges the fact that the Church 'has every right to claim that she is the pioneer, or even the author of African nationalism'[3] but on the other, he contends that because the Church is built on a prefabricated theology it has become vulnerable to the assault of the 'resurgence of the old gods'. He therefore asserts that the Church in Africa must be salvaged from a serious predicament through indigenisation. Idowu discusses this aspect of the paper in detail in another and perhaps earlier work, *Towards an Indigenous Church* (1965).[4] There he suggests that this predicament of the Church can best be resolved by training African personnel of quality and in appropriate numbers who would interpret the Christian Faith to their compatriots with a true sense of belonging. 'Today', he says, 'African leadership is inadequate both qualitatively and quantitatively'.[5] Idowu sets out the problem with reasonable perceptiveness even if we may not wish to subscribe to his language in every case.

We would say that, certainly within the last thirty years, with the development of nationalism and the collateral dissemination of the unclear term 'African personality' and its French counterpart *negritude*, the Church in Africa is faced with a clamant demand for

85

an interpretation of the Christian faith in a sanguine hope that such an interpretation when produced would provide a means of bringing home to Africans, the truths of the Christian Gospel in an idiom related to the African situation. We recall that William Vincent Lucas, Bishop of Masasi (1926–1944), had advocated a close relation between the infant Christian Church and the life of the tribe, without ignorantly accepting 'pagan standards and customs, (and) not realising the danger that lurks within . . .'.[6] Vincent Lucas deplored the fact that tribal life in some parts of Africa was disintegrating in favour of European ways of life. 'The whole world will suffer loss if the African forsakes the contribution he alone can make through striving to confine himself in moulds that are not his . . .'.[7] He therefore advocated the adoption of the 'rites and customs' of the people who were being converted into Christianity.[8] Vincent Lucas was born in 1883 and wrote these words as a result of his Masasi experience which began in 1926.

In West Africa, there was already a strong move in this direction. James Johnson the Sierra Leonean clergyman who had gone as a missionary to Nigeria in 1877, had anticipated Bishop Lucas by saying that the Church should be 'not an exotic but a plant become indigenous to the soil'. Johnson advocated 'a reform of the liturgy to suit local conditions'.[9] In 1886 Bishop Adjayi Crowther also reported on the use of 'native airs' at Otta in Yorubaland attributed to the immigrant catechist, James White who had served in Otta from 1854 to 1890. Indeed Professor J.F. Adjayi records a report by the Rev. Henry Townsend on the Otta Native airs in 1857.[10]

Similar attitudes were held by other West African Christians. Dr Edward Blyden in a speech delivered in 1876 refers approvingly to the remark made by Johnson to the effect that 'as the African Church failed once in North Africa in days gone by, so it will fail again, unless we read the Bible in our own native Tongue'.[11] Earlier, Blyden himself, arguing on the basis that there is 'a solidarity of human nature which requires the complete development of each part in order to (ensure) the effective working of the whole', had stated that Africans 'can attain to a knowledge of science, receive intellectual culture, acquire skill to develop the resouces of their country, and be made "wise unto salvation", without becoming Europeans'.[12] Elsewhere he infers that 'if Christianity is to take root at all in Africa, or to be to the native anything more than a form of words',[13] then two collateral policies should be pursued that is, first, a 'wholesome interference' with the ancestral organism should be introduced 'from without' and second, the Africans should be so educated that the foreign ideas which are introduced 'should be so assimilated as to develop and be fertilized by, native energy'.[14]

We would therefore confidently say that from 1854 onwards, although there seems to have been no evidence of any profound theological education among them, West African Christian leaders, lay and clerical had felt and indeed initiated schemes to indigenise the Christian faith. In recent times, there have been a plethora of advocates for the adaptation of Christian theology to worship. Professor E.B. Idowu, already referred to, has been one of the most vocal. The Rev T.E. Beetham, formerly Africa Secretary of the Methodist Mission Headquarters in London, writing in 1967 refers in sharp language to the slowness of the Church 'in becoming an African Church in worship and theological understanding'.[15] Beetham recognises that there is only one 'eternal Word of God, unchangeable', and therefore there 'can then be only one theology' but he goes on to say, 'The Word becomes incarnate for each generation and if it is in every generation to be 'touched and handled' so as to be universally recognised it must be incarnate in the life of every people. In this sense, there is need for an African liturgy and an African theology. In this sense, then the Church has been slow to become African'.[16] It is in this context that the term African becomes truly germane. It was noted at the A.A.C.C. Ibadan Conference in January, 1958, that much had been and was being done by way of Africanising the Church; music, thank-offerings, uniforms, puberty and Confirmation rites, marriage and funerals were especially mentioned.[17] At the same time, the Report expressly suggested that there was 'a need for Christians to reconsider African beliefs about the ancestors in the light of the doctrine of the Communion of Saints'.[18] The same Report stressed the importance of 'Education into Christianity' to provide a mooring against the strains and stresses of the modern world.[19] Beetham writing nine years later positively refers to the immense service already rendered by the Church of Africa both through the education provided by Christian Schools and by the fellowship created and sustained among African Christians. But he also recognises that the contemporary concern is how far can the worshipping community of Christians continue in post-independent Africa to exist and be an activating leaven in society. So he asks, with West Africa specially in mind, 'Have the roots of the Christian Community gone sufficiently deep in African society, with its traditional belief in the Supreme God and the spirit-world, its ritual for purification and consequent protection of individuals from harm within the family and clan? Has it a continuing place in that society as it now responds to the joint demands of national- ism and bureaucratic technology'?[20] A ready answer is not easily attainable.

2. THE INFLUENCE OF THE INDEPENDENT CHURCHES

Many writers, both European, American and African turn to the Independent Churches for an answer. These groups we are told practise healing, divination and prophecy on the one hand and stress faith in God on the other. Indeed, they seem to be drawing large numbers of Christians from the historic Churches to themselves. Dr. D.B. Barrett's (1968) figures stagger the reader.

Western Africa	938,600
Northern Africa	12,000
Southern Africa	3,719,000
Central Africa	1,212,600
Eastern Africa	980,000
TOTAL	6,662,200[21]

Barrett believes that many factors account for the creation and growth of independency.[22] In some cases, the basic causes for the growth of these independent Churches are theological, not religious factors usually unknown to the participants. But Harold Turner, known for his study of the Aladura Churches, sees these movements 'as primarily spiritual and religious movements striving for cultural integrity and spiritual autonomy; they are a creative response to the breakdown of old forms of African society by the formation of new groups for providing fellowship, security and some sanctions and guidance for the living.'[23] Harold Turner in his monumental two-volume work on the Aladura Movement gives a full account of 'the essentially African form of the Church' in terms of worship, the training and ranks of the ministry, a concern for water, the position of women, and the battle with the world of evil spirits; 'Africanisms and Africanisations abound'.[24] It contains within itself the total African tradition with an emphasis on community life.[25] In one sense, according to Turner the independent Churches are the 'end-products of Christian missions in Africa', but in another, 'they represent new

Christian beginnings . . . '.[26] He therefore affirms that the Aladura Church is African, yet universal, possessing the notes of the true church in a way 'similar to the historic creeds and formulations'.[27] At the same time, he frankly admits that the Aladura Church is 'devoid of theological or historical understanding'.

Turner's formula of 'Africanisms and Africanisations' abounding in the Aladura Church is true of all the other Independent Church Sects. He rejoices in the thought that independent churches are a creative growing point for the faith in Africa. He recognises potential dangers but 'it is at the danger point . . . that a true African theology will be born, not out of any syncretism, but out of understanding.' So Beetham is right when he complains of the slowness of the historic churches in becoming an African Church; but the additional phrase, 'in worship and theological understanding', thus introduces a criterion not readily applicable to the independent churches, according to Turner. We would therefore agree with G.C. Oosthuizen that 'all efforts to relate Christianity to the 'soil' in Africa are overdue'.

It is indeed interesting to recall that at the First Assembly of the A.A.C.C. in Kampala in 1963, special attention was given to the selfhood of the Church. The Report openly asserts that the Church in Africa has not attained selfhood. The reasons given may be summarised as follows:

(1) There is a multiplicity of Churches in Africa; using Barrett's figures it refers to 5,000 independent church movements which have emerged since 1862 'in thirty-four African nations and colonies with, in 1967, an estimated seven million (7,000,000) adherents . . .'. Add to these the multiplicity of Pentecostal Churches from the United States of America, the seventh-Day Adventist Groups, and the variety of Churches allied to the historic Churches and we have a long tale of disharmony.

(2) Christians walk along two ways – the old and the new. Indeed Christianity is still a foreign religion hence the independent churches are indicative of a 'more honest unsophisticated rebellion' against the form of Christianity introduced by the missionaries.

(3) The Church in Africa is built on 'hot-house' conditions provided by a 'well-planned organization for the Christian nurture of Africans'.

(4) The Church deals in foreign, prefabricated theology, which has, unfortunately, not grown out of the life of a living Church in Africa.

(5) There has developed a faulty theology of the Church which 'has resulted in a lack of a sense of sacrificial giving'.

(6) The Church in Africa trained teachers 'without giving them a sufficient intellectual and spiritual training so that they could question' their faith 'for themselves'.[28]

Professor Idowu's voice rings out clearly.[29] The Conference therefore called for 'an adequate and clear theology' and the development of African liturgies born out of 'the devotional experience of the Church'.[30]

Meanwhile we have the serious problem that with the rise of African nationalism, Christianity as proclaimed within the historic churches, is regarded as a 'white man's religion', associated with the now out-dated colonialist Powers. In the rapid social change which has come upon Africa the churches must therefore stop and examine their own position. The demand for such an examination is truly urgent.

Th. Müller-Kruger seeks to enunciate the problem in Asia–Africa by suggesting that in the West 'the concern is for a reform of theological education in order to restore the relevance of theology for the Church. In Asia and Africa . . . the concern is not with a reform of theological instruction, because no really standard form has yet emerged'. He goes on: 'The Churches still scarcely sense any need for an intellectual clarification and re-evaluation of their situation'. Müller-Kruger then suggests that the time has come for a 'theology of Missionary Encounter'. This means that theology should have an 'understanding of the Christian message which steps into the cultural environment and seeks to know and to understand this environment in its essence'. This process demands the establishment of bridges 'for the transmission of the theological goods'. So the traditional culture must be studied side by side with the impact of modern secularism, with a view to ensuring that theological study is carried out in the indigenous soil. Müller-Kruger's bridges can of course only be built on the results of careful and profound research. Müller-Kruger's interesting article was written in 1965.[31]

We recall here the note of warning sounded by Hans-Jürgen Greschat, who states that Historians of Religions 'should . . . shift the emphasis of religious research in Africa away from the study of exotic particulars, away from gods, institutions, rituals and concepts towards an understanding of the religiousness of persons'.[32] But what constitutes the exotic and to whom?

3. SOME CRITERIA FOR SELFHOOD

We would summarise the proceding discussion by saying that there is in West Africa, for example, a long standing record of attempts to adapt Christian worship to the African environment. The Nigerian airs already referred to and the increasing use of African music-patterns in some other countries testify to this claim. The independent churches, of course, with dancing and drums provide the examples which attract popular attention. But worship and theology go together. Harold Turner adopts language which suggests that 'African theology will be born not out of any syncretism but out of understanding'. Understanding of what? Here Th. Müller-Kruger's bridges and the implied bridgeheads come into prominence. Such bridges and bridgeheads on which theological understanding could be established demand a close and intimate study both of the religious life and thought-forms of the several African peoples as well as of the New Testament. The present writer holds the view that such understanding is not attainable by a direct jump from the natural theology of African rites and their associated myths to the deep notions contained in the New Testament without the influence of the Old Testament revelation. Harold Turner has, fortunately for us, provided instances of the lack of a sound Christian point of view in the Aladura Church on the ideas associated with God, Jesus Christ and the Holy Spirit to choose three principal topics. He therefore observes that they fail to grasp the notion that God is not only 'one and universal, almighty and righteous, yet loving and merciful', but also holy and righteous. The God whose glory makes him the God of history seems not to be understood by them. So he makes the comment that 'while the Church of the Lord emphasizes the severity of the judgement of God and reverences him with awe, it has hardly felt the full biblical sense of his holy righteousness when sin can still be dealt with merely by repentance and without atonement'.[33] We would of course wish Turner had gone on to explain how sin could be dealt with merely by repentance and without atonement according to the New Testament. Similar references to defects in the ideas held by the Aladura about Jesus Christ are noted by Turner. According to Turner, Jesus Christ 'seems to be cast in the role of the traditional African intermediary, who preserves due order in our approach to God, and at most may try to help us; he is far removed from the Christian concept of the mediator, who not only provides communication but also removes the barriers of sin and guilt that separate man from God'.[34] Indeed Jesus is thought of primarily in terms of the 'speaker' or of the ancestors or minor divinities 'who are links between men in this world and the gods beyond'.[35] We recall a like comment about the women of Johannesburg by Mia Brandel-Syrier that for them, 'the status of Jesus amongst the ancestors and other spirits is not clear. He may have become ranged next to the ancestors, and if over and above these, then possibly only in His role as the strongest wonder-worker'.[36]

According to Turner Jesus Christ is more a symbol of power through his rising from the dead to the Aladura Church. Of course, God is himself power whom no power can overcome.

Again in relation to the Holy Spirit, because of what Turner calls 'an impoverished conception' of Jesus Christ, in spite of the strong pneumatological aspects of the Aladura Church, the Spirit is 'thought of simply as the Spirit of God, as the way in which God is present in power in the individual and in the Church'.[37]

Two other topics call for brief mention. First *Sacrifice*, which for the Christian is supremely manifest in the Sacrifice of Jesus. To the Aladura, 'Prayer is Sacrifice'. Turner says that the sacrifice of Christ is understood by the Aladura in terms of enduring persecution, hardship and suffering in loyalty to the faith. The Aladura thus fail 'to understand the vicarious nature of the sacrifice of Christ'. Turner alleges that the Aladura lack 'interest in the sufferings or death of Christ'.[38] They seem to hold 'an attenuated form of the moral influence theory of the atonement' even if 'it contains seeds of development'.[39]

Second, their attitude to Man is equally defective, because of the defective grasp of the Person and Work of Jesus Christ. Sin is thought of in terms of the judgement of God but they have a faulty grasp 'of the full Christian idea of sin and forgiveness'.[40]

Man is of course surrounded by enemies; 'his vitality and power are undermined more by these evil forces than by his own sin and weakness. At the same time, the reality and magnitude of his demonic realm is not allowed to absolve men from personal responsibility for their own sin'. But the seriousness of human sin when silhouetted against the holiness of God is not fully grasped.

These and other flaws in the religious life of the Aladura make it unlikely that the advocates of African Theology can truly use the independent churches as their yardstick. It therefore seems inadvisable to accept Hans Jurgen Greschat's call for a shift of emphasis from the study of exotic particulars towards an understanding of the religiousness of persons in the attempt to arrive at an African Theology.

The Aladura attitude to Jesus Christ in particular reminds us of the important comment of Fred Welbourn that 'the difference between the old gods (of pagan Africa) and the God of Christianity is far greater than the difference between g and G. They cannot be measured against one another'.[41] We would add 'at the same time, many converts to Christianity find themselves struggling with a conflict of loyalties'. In a lecture given by Professor John Mbiti in 1969 at the Annual Meeting of the Christian Churches Educational Association on Christian Education in the background of African Tribal Religions, he cites a student who is quoted as having said:

'There are times when the Christian belief confuses me because it was only last year that my grandmother got very sick. No doctor could cure her and although she is a Christian she decided to contact a witchdoctor. The doctor gave her some medicines and also said that there was someone bewitching her but he promised to deal with the person severely. How my grandmother believed this and after having taken the medicine she was restored back to her normal self. How should I call this evil because my religious teacher told me that I should not believe in such things or should I call it good because it cured my granny when the Christian or foreign doctors had failed'.

4.   THE CASE FOR A THEOLOGIA AFRICANA

Here we have the crux of the matter of an African Theology. We would first of all emphasise that the term is somewhat misleading as in its current usage. We live in a world of epithets; it must be recalled that Tertullian, Cyprian and others were associated with an African Theology in the second and third centuries of the Christian era. The advocates of African Theology from Diedrich Westermann onwards think of African theologians as the interpreters of Christian theology in a way different from that possible to foreign theologians. But as one listens to discussions on African Literature in English one tends to become increasingly sceptical about the use of the term African in these contexts. Many Europeans write articles and books in English, sometimes with a distinctive style which marks them off from a native English writer. But these books are never referred to as German or Czech Literature in English. On the other hand, there seems to be a case for saying that Africans understand the culture of the soil on which they are nurtured better than most foreigners would.

We would accept Dr Mulago's thesis that common ground exists between Christianity and the African traditional religious thought-forms in, for example, the belief in the one Supreme Being as the Source, 'first source' of life, who cares for all his creatures, because

He is their Father.[42] But this is only one area of theological discussion. A Christian Theologian who seeks to use the ingredients of the 'African soil' to build a theology designed to meet the African situation must recognise the place of spirits – ancestral and otherwise – in the African world-view. Here we are confronted with a miscellany of rites and religious practices which have become the determining factors of the life of the average man and woman. So indeed whilst like the Christian, African peoples for the most part believe in one Supreme Being, at the same time He is not the principal directing agent of the historical factors of life. There are other areas which have to be carefully examined if African theology is to be intended to translate the Christian and, therefore, Biblical Concept of God and Creation, Man, sin and redemption, Jesus Christ, Son of God and Mediator, the Holy Spirit and the Church, for example.

In a yet unpublished Paper presented to the Theology Faculty Conference for Africa by the Lutheran World Federation, by the Finnish Theologian Raimo Harjula, Professor of Systematic Theology at the Lutheran Theological College at Makumira, Tanzania, the author pleaded for a Theologia Africana, which should seek to explore the 'African heritage' in the light of Christian communication. He listed a number of topics to be included in such exploration: e.g.

(a) Traditional ideas of Creation, Fall and Man
(b) Traditional beliefs and ideas concerning death and 'life after death'.
(c) African concept(s) of time and Christian eschatology
(d) Traditional offerings and sacrifices; their 'doctrinal' or 'philosophical' background
(e) Witchcraft and sorcery
(f) Traditional healing and the Healing Ministry of the Church,

in addition to the basic ideas held on the Supreme Being.[43]

Harjula interestingly, even if indirectly, leads us to consider the criteria, if one could use the term, which should guide the production of a Theologia Africana in the present context.

If indeed as Tom Beetham points out there is only one 'eternal Word of God, unchangeable' and therefore there 'can then be only one theology' which has to be made incarnate in the African situation, then care must be taken to ensure that African versions of the basic biblical teachings are not devised to produce a format approvingly plausible to those who have decided views on what should be African. We shall mention two approaches. First, Bishop

Bengt Sundkler, for example, in spite of his grasp of the African independent churches seems to have a preferential yardstick constructed out of the prevalence of Creation Myths, the popularity and perhaps ready applicability of the Old Testament to African life and customs, and the 'clan of community of the Living and the Dead'.[44] So dreams become vital factors in the assessment of the mental make-up of the African pastor and layman alike – but more so in the case of the pastor's call to the ministry.

Second, Fred Welbourn has, starting from a psychological argument drawn a distinction between 'guilt' and 'shame'.[45] Both may have an internal or an external reference, but they are different in content. Welbourn adopts the definition of guilt-feelings 'as arising from knowledge of a prohibition touched or transgressed, and of shame-feelings as response to a goal not reached'.[46] He associates these responses with 'tradition-directed' societies and with 'inner-directed' societies respectively, the latter being more puritanic in its influence. So members of tradition-directed societies tend to project to mystical beings much for which men who are inner-directed would assume personal responsibility. The discussion opens out interestingly as Welbourn develops his theme. There is a fundamental difference between the approach of Welbourn and Sundkler respectively to the ingredients of the African 'soil'. Welbourn could reasonably be described as adopting a philosophical attitude to a fundamental socio-religious factor of human society. Sundkler on the other hand uses a mythopoeic approach to attribute to psychic phenomena an explanation of the vocation to the Christian ministry, in particular, and the christian way of life in general. We would therefore go on to propose that if any Theologia Africana is to be cultivated, Welbourn's approach and not Sundkler's will serve the desired purpose; that is to say, an African theology must be built on a philosophical basis. Of course we take it for granted that every care must be exercised to ensure that the biblical doctrines are fully understood and adequately taught, to African Christians. At the same time, we take the view that the real exercise in translating Christian ideas into forms intelligible to the African lies in the area of *systematic* theology. No doubt Church History must be given special attention and must be related to local history to become truly intelligible. But systematic theology *per se* will provide the platform for the confrontation of the great Christian 'doctrines of creation, redemption, Christology, pneumatology, ecclesiology and eschatology' with the 'thought-worlds and world-views of the environment'. At the same time, we must be careful not to make difficult statements like Turner's reference to 'the full biblical sense of his (God's) holy righteousness when sin can still be dealt with merely by repentance and without atonement'.

To illustrate from West Africa. In order to interpret the Christian doctrine of regeneration to the Akan, one must according to Dr. J.B. Danquah seek to understand the emphasis laid on birth and life, with death as a transition phase. An intensive study of the subject in that context might readily shed fresh light on the traditional assumptions of Western theologians with regard to the Fall. Again, a close study of the ideas of life after death might lead to fresh ideas on the doctrine of purgatory, mortal and venial sin, and related questions like, Where do the dead go? Is reincarnation a Christian concept? How do we interpret original sin as taught in Western Christendom to Africans who believe that the human soul is pure and devoid of sin?

A Theologia Africana based on sound philosophical discussion need therefore not be a 'native' product, but a searching investigation into the content of traditional religious thought-forms with a view to erecting bridgeheads by which the Christian Gospel could be effectively transmitted to the African peoples. One area which is perhaps most promising in this regard is the Community. The African sees himself as part of a cultic community – a community which is incomplete without the supernatural world.[47] The worship of the ancestors, the attitude to birth and death, sin, sickness, forgiveness and health all converge on the central role of the community. Here doctrine and liturgy interesect and the role of the Church as a worshipping community with a message and mission can be made real both to Christians who are already within as well as to those outside the faith. We do not feel able to accept the comment that 'Liturgy as an aim in itself and the relative separation of religious life and morality . . . may well remain distinctive traits of African Christianity'.[48] In the so-called primitive West African communities we have studied, there is no distinctively separate 'religious life and morality' which could be identified as having been carved out from a greater complex of behaviour. Instead, the communal life is one coherent complex including work, legal and social obligations blended with religion and morals. We think Fred Welbourn is nearer the mark when he says, 'Most men . . . find the meaning and purpose of their lives in membership of a community; but the chief function of their "religion" is to keep that community intact'.[49] In other words, we would make the suggestion that the real value of a Theologia Africana is more likely to be one of *function* than of strictly *new content*. The universal theology of the Christian faith will and must always remain one; but interpreted in terms of the African soil, a Theologia Africana might correct the present imbalance caused by the stress on Historical Theology among many western theologians.

We would however end with two notes of caution. First, a Theologia Africana must avoid any over-readiness to adopt African indigenous ideas and practices merely because they fascinate foreign theologians on the one hand, or on grounds of nationalistic patriotism, on the other.

It is to the credit of Harold Turner that he can say that the Aladura church is devoid of theological and historical understanding even if we do not believe that Turner truly describes their outlook. And yet one is almost left with the impression that he believes that the members of the independent churches are moving along safer lines of advance than other Africans who are struggling to discover more appropriate means of evangelism within the historic churches.[50]

Second, whilst African theologians must be sensitive to the difficulties created by the so-called 'importation' of western theology and liturgy into Africa, they should at the same time adopt a constructive attitude through careful study and a realistic appraisal of the material they investigate in the African environment. This appraisal must also be backed by an open-minded attempt to study both the biblical teachings and the philosophical discussions of the doctrinal affirmations. A Theologia Africana must be part of the mainstream of the tradition of the Church whilst attempting to bring fresh insights into man's understanding of the work of God.[51] Dr. Eric James makes two comments which are relevant to this discussion.

First, that the Church has not a past history but it now is this history.[52]

Second, Theology is not the logos of man about God. Because of the incarnation of the Logos, theology is not primarily what man thinks about God in an abstract way, but rather what God has done and is doing for man.[53]

It is in this context that we would deplore any attempt to define a Theologia Africana as specifically devised and produced for Africans *per se*. In spite of the stir caused by the appearance of James H. Cone's *Black Theology and Black Power*, the book fails to provide any fresh theological insights. It does of course condemn racism as demonic and evil and advocates practical expressions of Christian love. 'All men are worthless apart from God's love', and 'all are worthy simply because God loves them' declares the writer.[54]

But the whole book is, on the one hand, a sustained declamation

97

of a Christian or so-called Christian society in which whites dis-
criminate against blacks and, on the other, a plea for the recognition
of the negro, *per se*, as a human being of equal value to all other
human beings and to Christians, in particular, in the sight of God.
So the writer says, 'in a white racist society, Black Theology believes
that the biblical doctrine of reconciliation can be made a reality only
when white people are prepared to address *black* men as black
men and not as some grease-painted form of white humanity'.[55]
Indeed, 'the task of Black Theology is to make the biblical message
of reconciliation contemporaneous with the black situation in the
United States of America'.[56]

We would therefore lay stress on the fact that a Theologia Africana
must not be based on such contemporary factors brought about as in
the United States of America by men who seem to be scarcely aware
of the sufferings of their fellowmen, may be because of a desire to
preserve an undesirable social distinction purely on the basis of the
colour of the skin of their less favoured compatriots.

Finally, a Theologia Africana is liable to suffer from the serious
defects of a global generalisation which covers a yet incompletely
chartered continent which on a diagram can embrace Japan, India,
Europe, New Zealand, U.S.A. (without Alaska) all the islands in the
Caribbean and Iceland.[57] The political criterion of citizenship by
birth or adoption also excludes many who, like the Asians of Kenya,
may truly feel they belong to Africa. We would therefore go on to
adopt the suggestion that the term '"African" is primarily a mytho-
logical term, expressive of love for a continent or commitment to an
ideal'.[58] Here lies the basis for African Unity. For Christians, the
religion of Jesus Christ is the only hope for unity among all men,
African or otherwise. A Theologia Africana should therefore provide
a common medium by which Africans and non-Africans, but even
more so, the multiplicity of Christian groupings could begin to think
together, first in the African continent and may be, in the providence
of God, in other parts of the world. In an age of Christian ecumenical
thinking, a Theologia Africana might very well be the means of making
Christians of various groups, think together and so worship together.
Christian witness might thus become truly effective at the village level
as well as in the large townships. It could provide the bridge by which
Christianity in Africa can be both African and yet universal.

5. CONCLUDING SUMMARY

Christianity in Africa naturally bore and still bears the marks of those
who introduced it into Africa. At the same time, for various reasons,

including the assumed superiority of the culture of the West, little attention was paid by the early missionaries to the religious thought-forms and practices of the African peoples. Christian African leaders seem however not to have felt fully at home with the 'imported' forms of worship. Today, African Christians and missionaries alike are calling for an intensive study of the ingredients of the indigenous religious thought-forms and practices in order to ensure a truly effective communication of the Gospel. So drums and dancing, the offering of sacrifices to the gods and to the ancestors are receiving greater attention. It is reasonable to suggest that with the emergence of independent African States, nationalistic feelings may be behind the trenchant criticisms of contemporary Christian teaching and worship.[59]

In spite of the difficulties inherent in the term African, there is a strong case for a Theologia Africana which will seek to interpret Christ to the African in such a way that he feels at home in the new faith. The independent churches have pointed the way to adaptations of Christian worship to suit the African world view. But in their present stage of development, no clear theological thinking has yet been evolved by them. Care must therefore be exercised to avoid both syncretistic tendencies as well as a hollow theology for Africa. To the present writer, the answer lies in the rigorous pursuit of systematic Theology, based on a philosophical appraisal of the thought-forms of the African peoples.[60]

THE BASIS OF A THEOLOGY FOR AFRICA

In his book *The Christian Ministry in Africa*,[1] Dr. Bengt Sundkler includes a chapter entitled 'Towards Christian Theology in Africa', in which he provides the reader with much thought-provoking material. Using illustrations drawn from the entire continent, he makes some important suggestions which deserve careful consideration, and which may be summarised here as follows:

1. He posits that 'theology in Africa has to interpret . . . Christ in terms that are relevant and essential to African existence'; this means that it 'must needs start with the fundamental facts of the African interpretation of existence and the universe' (p. 281). These facts are, of course, found in the various tribal myths, which almost invariably relate to the Beginning of Things, to Creation and to the development of clan and tribal life. They form the matrix of the African's world-view, and so of his reality. Dr. Sundkler therefore goes on to advocate a careful study of African myths as they 'constitute an "original revelation", which is re-enacted in annually recurrent festivals, in a rhythm which forms the cosmic framework of space and time' (p. 282). Alongside this emphasis on the Beginning of Things, Dr. Sundkler notes the equally important attention that Africans give to what he calls 'the clan community of the Living and the Dead'. Accordingly, he isolates two themes as the most promising basis for an African contribution to Christian theological thinking: firstly, those emphases which appear to be 'the fro foci of the theological encounter in Africa' – the beginning of mankind and of the people of God, and the clan community of the living and the dead – and secondly, the Church and its ministry.

Dr. Sundkler is prepared to admit a parallelism between the great Hebrew stories and the African myths, and says that this parallelism 'helps to elucidate the significant reaction of African preachers to the Old Testament. The Old Testament in the African setting is not just a book of reference. It becomes a source of remembrance' (p. 285).

100

Thus, 'the stories of Genesis offer more to the African preacher and theologian than to the Westerner'. Similarly, the rhythmic pattern of the African's thought and life will help to make the Eucharistic anamnesis 'a re-calling of representation of the Body and Blood of Christ' (p. 286).

Speaking of the links between the living and the dead, Dr. Sundkler observes that 'the clan is the link between the generations living on earth and the generations in their existence as ancestors'. In his judgment, this emphasis on the family will prove to be the basis of the African's ecclesiology, enabling him the more readily to grasp the concept of the Church as the Great Family. African theologians will likewise feel a concern for the dead 'and the meaning of their life, or death' (p. 289), and will give due attention to the 'stark realities of Suffering (social and physical), Sickness and Death'.

2. Regarding the development of a theology of the Church and the ministry, Dr. Sundkler is well aware of the gaps in 'patterns of church life brought by Protestant missions from Europe and America'.

> It appears that Protestant Christianity was brought to Africa by nineteenth century Pietism, Puritanism and Evangelicalism, and twentieth-century Holiness and Pentecostal groups. While these historical expressions of Christianity made lasting contributions to the evangelisation of the African masses, their strongest impact lay elsewhere than in the ecclesiological field. As Western individualists, the missionaries representing these groups had not always sufficient understanding of the corporate nature of the Church and still less, perhaps, and appreciation of the supra-individual and corporate forces which are at work in African group life (p. 296).

He goes on to comment that 'the great Biblical terms of the Church – the People of God, the Body of Christ, the Household or Family of God – find a vibrant sounding-board in the structure of African social patterns, particularly of the clan'. Dr. Sundkler believes that the festivals of the Church's year contribute to the corporate fellowship of the Church, for they are all occasions of 'remembrance', and he stresses the need for a fresh discovery of the connexion between ecclesia and leitourgia (p. 302, cp. p. 287). He then refers with exceptional clarity to the minister as the mid-man between God and the congregation, the one man who can best hold the congregation together as well as bring them in prayer and devotion to the throne of God.

All African theologians interested in the shape of African Christianity must feel grateful to Dr. Sundkler for his lucid and precise presentation of this theme. But as one reads the book one cannot but wonder at times whether he has not overrated the impact on the thought forms of African peoples of 'the two foci of a future theological encounter'. Granted that the African myths relate to the Beginning of Things and therefore provide material for what he has called 'an original revalation', has he not fore-shortened the total *raison d'etre* of the Old Testament? Indeed the African myths reflect the P-story of Creation as well as attribute the origin of sickness and death to man's disobedience to the will of God. The Temne of Sierra Leone, for instance, have both aspects in their tribal myths; and the Kposso say that leprosy is the result of the disobedience of a man, Sropa by name, when ordered by God not to go near the fire that He had created. No doubt Africans who read the biblical accounts will readily silhoutte them against their own indigenous stories. But will they necessarily pass on to the Hebrew concept of history? When Dr. Sundkler asserts that the Old Testament becomes to the African 'a source of remembrance', we must ask, Remembrance of what? Has he not ignored the important fact that 'primitive' man sees life as of extra-human origin – what Mircea Elaide has called 'the Myth of the Eternal Return'? Elaide states that primitive man's behaviour:

> is governed by belief in an absolute reality opposed to the profane world of 'unrealities'; in the last analysis, the latter does not constitute a 'world' properly speaking; it is the 'unreal' par excellence, the uncreated, the non-existent: the void.[2]

In other words, 'the man of the traditional civilizations accorded the historical event no value in itself; . . . he did not regard it as a specific category of his own mode of existence'.[3] If the Hebrew concept of history as the unfolding of the gracious purpose of God is to be passed on to African Christians, their myths do not provide a basis on which to build. This 'mnemic theology' is in our judgment fraught with great dangers.

Again, while it is natural that 'the clan community of the Living and the Dead' will occupy the attention of the African theologian, Dr. Sundkler has not mentioned that there must be a clarification of the ways in which the ancestral dead of African communities are in fact guardians of the moral life of the clan. This is a matter of some importance, because in every African community the ancestral dead are regarded as co-guardians with the totemic spirits of the mores of their clans.

Finally, in spite of his able presentation of the minister as the midman between God and man, Dr. Sundkler omits any specific reference to the potential influence of the Christian priest as a necessary off-set of the pagan priests. These men, such as the Ifa priests so well portrayed by Dr. Idowu in his recent book *Olodumare*,[4] abound in Africa and they minister with due devotion to the needs of the people, as mid-men between them and the various totemic spirits they venerate. In this connexion, we should have been grateful to Dr. Sundkler if, when discussing the Eucharistic anamnesis as a 're-calling or representation of the Body and Blood of Christ', he had gone a stage further to stress the significance of the 'sacrificial' content of the Eucharist. Sacrifice is inescapable in the African environment. It is the cardinal factor of African religious practices. A comment by Eva Meyerowitz is relevant here. She tells us that for members of the Ntorɔ cult in Ghana, 'a prayer and the sacrifice of a fowl to the husband's ntor were thought sufficient to procure a child'; only if the woman was unable to conceive was she sent to pray to 'whatever god she chose'. She then instances wives of kings and chiefs who made pilgrimages to various other 'renowned gods in foreign lands'. But she goes on to say:

> Today with the increased incidence of sterility arising from the spread of venereal disease, people, disappointed with their gods and with Christianity, are turning to foreign 'fetish' gods, introduced from the north, which promise by their magical powers to be more effective than Ntor.[5]

We would, however, fully endorse Dr. Sundkler's remark that 'theology in Africa has to interpret...Christ in terms that are relevant and essential to African existence' and that 'a theologian who with the Apostle is prepared to become...unto Africans as an African, must needs start with the fundamental facts of the African interpretation of existence and the universe'. Accordingly, we wish to suggest three possible lines of approach that are based on the life-setting and thought-world of the African.

1. A FULL TREATMENT OF THE INCARNATION

This should not be a mere repetition of the customary study of the Person and Work of Christ, so familiar in the traditional texts, but rather a treatment which embraces the notions of Christ as man, and so manifesting God's love to man. Into this must be woven God's share in human sufferings and God's victory over death and over all the disastrous influences which abound in man's everyday experiences. In short, it should be a study of Jesus Christ, born as I was, growing as I did, perhaps with all the innocent mischief characteristic of a growing boy or girl, persecuted by His contemporaries because He was fully dedicated to the service of God, and eventually dying because of His unflinching loyalty to God. And yet, God raised Him from the dead because He was 'that Man in whom God lived and acted (and still does act) humanwise'.[6] In such a context we could set a treatment of the Church as the Body of Christ or, in the words of Dr Sundkler, as 'the Great Family', comprehending all who are committed to Christ and who are accordingly in a mystical relation to him.

In this era of increasing national independence in Africa, there is an urgent need for Christians to cultivate the 'one man' in Christ (Gal. 3:28). Already the emergence of new states is creating a dimension of disparateness hitherto unknown. The many national flags, and the divagations of currencies and currency regulations, make it imperative that Africans should be helped to discover that they can all turn to the Church of Christ for its unifying comprehensiveness as the whole Christian Family. This is a factor that can readily displace the concept of the tribe and its various age-mate kinship groups. Carefully defined, the Body of Christ represents the *primum ens* from which all Christians take their origin. Here the tribe can give place to the whole community of the Church, with Jesus Christ as its first member. This is essentially a different and, we suggest, a more salutary approach than the concept of 'chief' which Paul Fueter, for example, has proposed in an otherwise interesting attempt to grapple with the application of Christian tenets to the African environment. He says, 'We preach Christ who is the real chief, the king of Africa. He is the ruler who comes and in whose presence all is forgotten, with whom one is secure for ever'.[7] We would suggest that the use of chiefship to describe an attribute of Jesus Christ is particularly vulnerable because:

1. Chiefs lost their pristine power and influence in the old colonial days; in the new independent states their positions are, generally speaking, quite precarious.

2. Chiefship does not *per se* imply unquestioned supreme rule; it never has. The Chief is always answerable to his council of elders, who in a measure determine his tenure of office.

3. The Chiefs of African tribesmen have never been readily accessible to the ordinary man. There has always been a middleman through whom the chief must be approached, except when he is approached not as chief, but as father. Such middlemen are known as *Okyeame* among the Akan, *Bangura* among the Temne of Sierra Leone, *Balogun* among the Yoruba, or *Lavale* (mouthpiece) among the Mende of Sierra Leone. Even gifts offered to the chief had to be sent through the middleman, who at court was the royal spokesman.

4. Again, chiefs generally live in a walled settlement and are therefore not exposed to ordinary contacts with their subjects. Thus, for example, the Alafin of Oyo wears a veil when he goes out on official circuits, and the King of Dahomey was never seen when having his meals.

Accordingly we feel that the concept of chiefship is unsuited to the Person of Christ. But to represent Jesus Christ as the first-born among many brethren, who together with Him form the Church, is truly in keeping with African notions. An effort must be made to bring home to Christians the mystical relation between Christ and the Christian of which St. Paul speaks in Galatians 2:19 ff.

An extended treatment of the Incarnation must include some discussion of the Church as a functioning Body and so of its ministry and the work of that ministry. We suggest that considerable emphasis should be given to the concept of Jesus Christ as God's Apostle, who also sent forth His disciples to 'go forth and preach the Gospel to the whole world'. This authority, we believe, has been handed down to the Church through its ministry. As Dr. Sundkler rightly observes, 'To many an African pastor, the link of his Church with the Church of the Apostle will afford the guidance he needs in order to understand his own ministry'.[8] This point of view will be rejected by a number of missionary leaders as a specially perverted attitude of some Anglicans. But in the African environment the skills of witch-doctors and cultic priests are known to be handed down either from father to son or from master to pupil. The Asentehene of Ghana is the example par excellence of such a legacy. He inherits the Golden Stool from his predecessor by a special rite of appointment, and de jure becomes ɔkmfo ɔhene (King or Chief of the Priests)'.[9] He is thus the 'supreme priest of his country for in his hands lies the cult of his departed ancestors and he represents the priests (ɔkmfo) in the state council'. Thus the implied doctrine of apostolic succession not only would not create any difficulty for African Christians, if they would admit it, but it is also part of their life-setting and thought-setting. The question of priest-craft, and the ancillary factors of 'confession', 'sacrifice' and 'absolution' as a remedy for sin, must also be associated with this notion. Eva Meyerowitz says of the Akan members of the Ntoro cult:

> If a person feels . . . that he has defiled his kra by a particular sin, he usually goes to a priest of whatever god he fancies. The priest then will act as his soul-bearer and induce him to sacrifice doves, the one creature 'nearest to Nyame' (p. 185, footnote 1).

Earlier she observes that a breach of the taboos of the Ntoro cult, described as a 'sin', 'carries its own punishment by making the culprit sick and finally driving him to his ntoro spirit to confess, pray and make a sacrifice' (p. 118). In this context, a theology for Africa must stress the Eucharistic Sacrifice as the means of eliminating and replacing every form of oblation and propitiation of the cultic spirits. Weddings, funerals and all the existing occasions on which the cultic priests are employed should accordingly include the One Oblation of Jesus Christ. In addition, an effort should be made to provide a sense of mystery such as is found in the various *rites de passage* and the many cultic rites that are so popular.

2. A DOCTRINE OF IMMORTALITY

Most African groups believe that the soul of an individual persists in one form or another after death. Either it climbs a steep hill where it will abide, or it crosses a river into another land (not necessarily physical). They believe also that after death the soul of a wicked person – a witch, for instance – is many times more dangerous than that of a living person. So the Temne of Sierra Leone used to dismember witches; the Efik burned them; some tribes in Nyasaland threw them to the hyenas, so that they might not be 'permitted to survive death'.[10] Similarly among the Kikuyu, a person who was known to practice Orogi – that is, one who had killed by poisoning a man, woman or child – was accused of witchcraft, tried, and, if found guilty, burnt.[11] There is also a queer belief that a person may be reincarnated in his grandchildren, and at the same time persist in the spirit world. But there is no suggestion of any idea akin to the Christian concept of 'eternal life' or of the Resurrection of the dead.

African theologians have the task of presenting to their fellow Christians the difficult concept of Resurrection, partially experienced in this life by all who are baptised into the Body of Christ, and fully realised after death. At the same time, Resurrection must not be confused with survival, for Resurrection implies the death of body, soul and spirit, and their later revival by the power of the Holy Spirit[12]. Here we are faced with several important questions, such as: What is the meaning of death? Does the soul or spirit die, and if so, how? Do the soul and the spirit die in the same way as the body? How do we interpret 'eternal death?' What do we mean by 'the Church Expectant' and 'the Church Triumphant'? What is the fate of those of our ancestors who died without accepting Jesus Christ? Does hell exist in terms of the mediaeval concept we have inherited from the West? What is the present role of our ancestral dead? These are questions that touch the roots of the African thought-world because we all believe in the existence of our ancestral dead. In the words of Dr. Baeta of Ghana 'Whatever others may do in their own countries,

106

our people live with their dead'.[13] Arising from these questions there is yet another: Should the Christian convert pray for the soul of his pagan ancestors? And if he does so pray, to what benefit is it?

3. A DOCTRINE OF THE OMNIPOTENCE OF GOD

In view of Dr. Sundkler's reference to an 'original revelation' among Africans, great care should be taken, first, to discover the true content of this revelation, and then to provide a carefully worked out statement of the Christian understanding of the character of God, as manifested in the person of Jesus Christ, the final revelation. In the first instance, the word 'original' is full of difficulties. Does it mean 'unique', and if so, what is the Christian revelation? Or does it mean 'primary' in point of evolution? If so, what is the basis of determining this primariness? Or is it a mutation different from anything which had gone before, but in fact an offshoot from the main stem? We find the term 'original' difficult to understand and, unless special qualities can be attributed to 'revelation' within the African continent, we would question its propriety.[14]

In most of Africa, God is postulated as the Creator of the world, but as now being far away from it. He lives in the sky, but once upon a time the sky was near to the earth and accessible to man. Unfortunately God had to remove Himself from such close proximity to man because of man's behaviour. Various myths in different parts of the continent give a number of versions of what happened. To-day, however, God is far removed from man, and so out of man's reach. But although the language used expresses physical distance, the real issue is one of psychological distance. God may not be directly approached. Only the intermediate spirits may be so approached, because in them only can the 'sacred' be clearly manifested. They are capable of action and may be invoked in times of need because they are regarded as originating from God and owing their power to Him.[15] Of course, God Himself may be invoked in times of national crisis, such as drought or famine. But this is not the practice in every part of Africa. The Kwotto of Northern Nigeria, for instance, invoke the ancestral chiefs and request them to convey the petitions of the people to God, on the ground that as chiefs they are *de jure* priests and in the line of succession of men who know how to represent man to God. As spirits, they can do this more efficiently. They are, moreover, in the direct line of descent from God, and nearer to His presence.[16]

At the same time, there is also an accepted idea that everything that happens occurs with the direct approval of God. On the one hand, it is believed that God is Judge and that He stands for social justice among men; and on the other hand, there is an equally strong belief that evil intentions are perpetrated only with the approval of God. Every man and woman, every event and every action, is subject to the all-supreme will of God. Thus both the man who strives to achieve a noble end and the fiend intent on perpetrating the most dastardly deed attain their goals each 'by the will of God'.[17]

First, we have the problem of what, in his book *Fear Fetish*, the late T.S. Johnson, Assistant Bishop in the Diocese of Sierra Leone, called 'the Permissive Will of God'.[18] Taken to its logical conclusion, this phrase implies that nothing ever happens unless directly or implicitly according to the will of God. Of course, if God is in sovereign control of the world, it is logical to conclude that He must exercise supreme authority over everything that happens in it. On the other hand, if this interpretation is conceded absolutely, various disasters, some physical and others caused by human self-assertiveness, must be closely examined. Perhaps it was appropriate in the early history of Israel that the great earthquake and consequent volcanic action that led to the destruction of Sodom and Gomorah should be attributed to the punitive action of God on account of the sinfulness of the inhabitants of those two cities. But in the light of that interpretation, how do we look upon the earthquake that swept Morocco three years ago in which 14,000 people in Agadir lost their lives in a matter of minutes? How do we explain the destruction of hundreds of thousands of innocent women and children at Hiroshima when the first atom bomb was dropped in 1945? What do we say of the perversity of Adolf Hitler and his supporters which led to the massacre in gas chambers of over six million Jews, and to the torture and slaughter at the hands of German soldiers of so many persons in Holland and Norway, for example, during the years of occupation? Again, how can it be said that God approved, or at least turned a blind eye, when one child was run over and killed by a passing motor car when several other children were also crossing the road at the same time?

On the face of it, this theory of the permissive will of God may provide a sense of consolation for some by its emphasis on the fact that God is always at the helm. It seems to fail, however, to take full account of the Christian teaching on the problem of evil – that evil exists as a condition of life at two levels, physical and moral. Our knowledge of geology teaches us that the earth in its physical composition is not perfect, and that earthquakes and volcanic eruptions are therefore a natural result of its present state. We know also that moral evil is contingent on man's freedom to choose and

108

act as he desires. As long as man feels free to choose, he is apt to set up a rival kingdom to God's, with himself at the centre. This is the problem of sin. Any other approach to this problem leads us to make God a scapegoat. Indeed, if the good man and the bad can both expect God to listen to and grant their requests, the resultant situation can best be described by the epigram Dilemma, written during World War I by Sir John Squire:

God heard the embattled nations sing and shout,
  'Gott strafe England!' and 'God save the King!'
God this, God that, and God the other thing.
  'Good God!' said God, 'I've got my work cut out'.[19]

It must be recognised that, in giving man the freedom to choose and to act on his own initiative, God has in fact restricted His own sovereignty as an act of grace. In addition, Christian teaching stresses that the omnipotence of God is manifested in symbols of love and not in demonstrations of physical power. This is attested by the fact that Jesus Christ came to the world as a manifestation of God's love. The fact that Jesus was born of a Virgin, and God's raising Him from the dead when sinful men had put Him to death, are unique instances of this omnipotence of love.

Secondly, the 'psychological distance' mentioned above indicates an emphasis on the transcendence of God, but this is not linked with any suggestion that He is holy. Majestas is associated almost entirely with the cultic spirits. Awe, reverence and holy fear are seen at their best in the various rites performed at the shrines.[20] Yet, except among the Akan of Ghana and perhaps the early Yoruba, there is no organised worship of God. There are no priests, no temples, no altars and no set rites in His honour. On the other hand, in matters of personal concern, or in times of grave personal distress, private individuals are known to direct their petitions to God without reference to any intermediaries. Thus among the Mende of Sierra Leone, a mother whose child is going away from home to live with another family will say, 'May God teach you to be discreet and to be wise'. Sleeping and waking are regarded as the direct result of God's influence. Persons with a grievance will, as a final resort, state their case to God in a personal address when there is no hope of reparation through the existing customary channels. God is transcendent but at the same time He is assumed to be capable of hearing the appeals of such people, and of giving them due redress. He is no doubt far away, yet sleeping and waking, discretion and healthy up-bringing, are all attributable to Him. There is, however, no real, living, personal relationship between man and God. God is assumed to be vaguely near, but no one knows how.

Christian theology therefore has a duty to African converts to present God as He whose Name is holy, who dwells in the high and lofty place, but with him also who is of a humble and contrite heart, through the mediation of Jesus Christ. Thus Jesus Christ, rather than the ancestral of cultic spirits, will be the means of direct contact with God. He will become the site of 'the holy' (an aspect familiar in the rites connected with the various spirits), but He will also become the focus of the personal relationships so lacking in the pagan rites.

Finally, it seems true to say that the ancestral and cultic spirits provide demonstrable or perceptible symbols of the omnipotence of God. If they must be ousted completely from the religious life of the African, it must be in terms of the personal relationships which are implicit in the pagan approach to the Supreme God. For the Christian, these relationships are quite explicit: they are based on God's grace. We may therefore seek to present God along these lines: first, as Creator, Lord, King, Father and Judge; and secondly, in terms of dynamic symbols, as the source of life and light, spirit and wisdom, love and sacrifice – terms which are readily understood by Africans, but now filled with Christian significance. Into this framework, then, we may work a doctrine of the Trinity – God as Creator and Father, as Redeemer and Saviour, and as Sanctifier and Inspirer. In such a framework the basic concepts of God's transcendence and His immanence become real, through the personal mediation of Jesus Christ and the continuing influence of the Holy Spirit.

Any treatment of the omnipotence of God must ultimately lead to a discussion of Christian worship. In the context of Africa, this will especially concern sacrificial worship, which is the chief content of all pagan African worship.[21] Two points may be noted here. First, by presenting Jesus Christ as the first-born among many brethren, we install him at the place where, in pagan African religious life, the ancestral and cultic spirits once predominate. So the awe, the reverence and holy fear, the sense of devotion, the abandon and the obedience, which are so markedly part of the cultic rites, will naturally pass to the worship of Jesus Christ, together with that sense of the holy which is generally absent in pagan references to God. Again, whereas in pagan worship the cultic shrines and altars are limited to the rites associated with the spirits, the transfer of these altars to Jesus Christ will lead to a transfer, through Him, to the worship of God, because where Jesus Christ is, God is. The sacrifices offered by the priests will no longer be physical offerings or the

110

sacrifice of animal victims. They will be offerings of the One true Sacrifice of Himself once offered by Jesus Christ for the sin of the world.

Secondly, the ancestral and cultic spirits are believed to have a 'real presence' in the pagan rites. If they are to be replaced by Jesus Christ, such substitution can be truly effected only by another Real Presence at Christian rites, that is, at the Sacrifice of the Body and Blood of Jesus Christ at the Eucharist. The Eucharist must therefore be presented as the great occasion when the priest offers a sacrifice to the praise and glory of God's Divine Majesty, as a memorial of Christ's death and Passion, and in thanksgiving for the benefits which have come to man through the forgiveness of his sins. Such a sacrifice may be described in two parts: The Oblation of the Body and Blood of Christ, He Himself being the true High Priest; and the oblation of ourselves to God, through Christ, united with Him in the perfect offering.[22] Only when we present to God the perfect offering of Jesus Christ can we go on to offer ourselves also in Him, as a living sacrifice acceptable to God. To those of us who are Anglicans, the 1662 Book of Common Prayer seems woefully lacking in this aspect of the Eucharistic rite. This is a lack that must be remedied in any serious presentation of the Christian Sacrifice. To African Christians, Christ must be presented as the 'first-born' among many brethren, not in terms of space or time, but in terms of His representativeness of the human race. In Him we must live, and through Him we must pray that God shall be All in All.

SOTERIOLOGY VIEWED FROM THE AFRICAN SITUATION

The Christian message of Salvation is a proclamation of God's free offer to man through Jesus Christ of love unmerited by Him in spite of the intransigence created by Sin. Sin is essentially a revolt against God, man setting himself up in place of God. But in the Christian setting, God as King, instead of lining up the insurgents, condemning them of treason and bringing them to face a firing squad, came down in the person of Jesus Christ to remove the consequent alienation. Anger, yes! God was no doubt angry with man but he never became embittered against him. So He paid the price of suffering with Jesus Christ on the cross. 'God was in Christ reconciling the world unto himself, not reckoning unto them their trespasses, . . .' (2 Cor. 5:19). St. Paul goes further to assert that 'Him, (i.e. Jesus Christ) who knew no sin, he (God) made to be sin (Snaith would say, a sin-offering) on our behalf; that we might become the righteousness of God in him' (2 Cor. 5:21). So Leonard Hodgson says, 'The wrath of God and divine punishment are essential elements in a doctrine which is to face the facts of evil and retain a fundamental optimism'.[1] God's share in the exercise of defeating evil is naturally embodied in the cross. But God's Punishment always leaves room for Forgiveness. For Christians, this aspect of God's attitude to man must always be paramount in any discussion on our relations to Him. So Hodgson goes on to say, 'If in spite of our sins we are to believe that God remains good, that in the nature of things the last word lies with goodness and there is for us some hope of restoration, we must be assured that our sins have failed to affect His goodness by making Him either a partner in our evil deed or embittered and revengeful as a result of it. It is this assurance which the Christian Church is charged to proclaim to sinners in its preaching of the doctrine of atonement'.

But the effect of Christ's saving work is to redeem the whole man into sanctification. For Paul, the whole man consists of body, soul and spirit: 'The God of peace himself sanctify you wholly; and may

112

your spirit and soul and body be preserved entire . . . .' (1 Thess: 5:23). Milligan commenting on this passage draws attention to the Greek word, ὁλόκληρον, translated 'wholly'; it emphasises, he says, 'the several parts to which the wholeness spoken of extends, no part being wanting or lacking in completeness'. So he goes on to add 'the three subjects . . . are evidently chosen in accordance with the general O.T. view of the constitution of man to emphasise a sanctification which shall extend to a man's whole being, whether on its immortal, its personal, or its bodily side.'[2]

This Old Testament view of the constitution of man, divides him up into body, soul (*nephesh*) and spirit (*ruach*). Th. C. Vriezen understands *ruach* to mean 'the whole of the spiritual sentiments that animate man' and *nephesh*, as the 'personality', the 'individuality'. Indeed, 'the *nephesh*' is the vitality that animates the body . . .' Vriezen points out that the *ruach* though not said to be something divine in the Old Testament yet it returns to God[3] who gave it (Eccles. xii: 7). Elsewhere he refers to *ruach* as 'draught, current of air, wind, spirit' and to *nephesh* as 'movement of life', 'self', 'soul'.[4]

It is therefore in the context of this tripartite division of man that soteriology should be considered when thought of in respect of the African situation.

1. THE AFRICAN UNDERSTANDING OF THE CONSTITUTION OF MAN

Man is generally thought of as constituted of body and soul, but the soul can have a multiple content. The Akan of Ghana provide a good instance of this feature of the soul. Man, to the Akan, consists of the blood of the mother (*mogya*) a life-soul (*kra*) and a personality soul (*sunsum*) or later, *ntoro*. Margaret Field refers to the *kra* as 'soul' and to the *sunsum* as 'mind, spirit'.[5]

The *kra* is a spark of Nyame – the female aspect of the Supreme Deity – which is of the nature of fire and vivifies mother's blood as it flows in the foetus, thus imparting life to the baby. The *sunsum* or *ntoro* is father's contribution to the life of the baby and represents his individuality. These two spiritual elements of the human being must however live in harmony. The *kra* needs a good *sunsum* to provide a medium through which it may express itself and does not leave the body without causing sickness or death. In the latter case, it returns to the City of Nyankopon, the male aspect of the Deity, and renders an account of its performance in the incarnate life. The *sunsum* on the other hand may leave his body in dreams or in

113

mind-wandering states without ill-effects. So it is that part of the individual that assumes the role of a witch.[6]

Eva Meyerowitz makes the point that at a certain stage in the history of the Akan people the *kra* came to represent 'the immortal soul' and was contrasted with 'the mortal soul, conscious of itself, personality'.[7] Two points relevant to the present discussion therefore arises: First, because the *kra* is a spark of divinity each man 'is in direct touch with God'. It is therefore pure and is given a mission to fulfil in the life-time of the individual. Danquah says that if a *kra* fails to fulfil its mission in any one incarnation, it must come back to earth and be reincarnated along the matrilineal line. This process will continue until the *kra* becomes full of goodness.[8] The due accomplishment of this mission however depends on the right relationship between the *sunsum* and the *kra*. Any disharmony leads to sickness because, according to Debrunner, in such cases, 'the pure part wants to leave the impure'.[9] But this pure part according to Danquah is always the *kra*. No evil 'stains or singes its goodness, but evil can arrest its growth' to attain a fulfilment of its mission, *nkrabea*. He then goes on to say 'Evil . . . exists but only on the *sunsum* side'.[10] This relationship between body, soul and spirit may therefore be likened to a steam engine. The total machine is the engine. But its performance depends on (a) steam for its power and (b) the pistons etc. for movement. The steam is of course always pure but if the pistons are out of good repair then the steam is wasted and the engine loses potential power. All the time, the steam remains pure *in se*. Williamson therefore concludes that in respect of the Akan, 'As to man and his needs, the Akan interprets this, not in terms of sin but in vitalistic terms'.

Here we are at the crossroads. Williamson obviously overstates the case when he maintains that 'The Akan knows "no problem of sin" or "problem of suffering"'.[11] This use of *sin* implies sin against God as Christians understand the term and is related to the emphasis on guilt as we shall see later on. On the other hand, as will be demonstrated later, there is strong evidence which points to the fact that the Akan and for that matter other tribal Africans do have a concept of sin, albeit at a plane lower than that of the Christian concept. We would with Williamson say, however, that the Christian concept of Salvation cannot be equated with that of the Akan.

The position so briefly presented in respect of the Akan holds true of other West African groups, even when their ideas of the soul are not as fully categorized as, for example, among the Mende of Sierra

Leone and the Yoruba of Nigeria. Since, even for the Christian, salvation must in the final analysis lead to a removal of sin as an oppressive spiritual force (1 Cor. 15:59), let us now proceed to look into the African situation.

2. PATTERNS IN AFRICAN IDEAS OF SALVATION: PERSONAL AND COMMUNAL FACTORS

To be in a position to assess in what areas of life tribal Africans would seek salvation we will first of all seek to discover and set out some of the factors of life which they find oppressive or to which they must conform in order to live in harmony with themselves and their environment. In a short statement we would isolate

(A) VITAL-POWER, NATIVE AND ENVIRONMENTAL

Ranging from, say, the Mende of Sierra Leone to the Yoruba of Nigeria among other tribes in the vast continent of Africa, it is true to state that the tribal African, though not only he, believes that the world is peopled with demonic influences which include men-particularly sorcerers and witches – and evil supernatural beings, all of them manifesting *power*. This postulation of the supernatural originates of course from the externalisation and subsequent personalisation of cause and effect. When one suffers disappointments or frustrations, when a member of the family falls ill, or when a mother loses a number of children in succession, tribal man is apt to look for the reason why in a context outside that of physical cause and effect; no questions are raised in respect of his inability to fulfil his ambitions. For people who are exposed to wild beasts, poisonous snakes, the unpredictable alternation of droughts and floods, sickness and good health, rich harvests and poor crops, backed by a high infantile mortality, it is not too difficult to understand this postulation of external hostile agencies more powerful than man.

As Placide Tempels tells us, those experiences are all interpreted as instances of a diminution of power, each caused by the influence of another power greater than or hostile towards men. But man is in himself a '*power.*' So if one succeeds in any undertaking it is because 'one has a "power" of a higher order than the next man, a "power" of a higher order than the evil "wills" that permeate the world'.[12] Indeed, there tends to develop a notion, as among the Mende and

Kono, both of Sierra Leone, that such a one has 'witch-power' – it may be a cloak or some other object. Even the healing-doctors who cure their patients of illnesses attributable to witches are themselves believed to possess powers cognate with witchcraft albeit never used with evil intent, e.g. the Mende, *hu-bɔnε*.[13]

This vital power is however, subject to fluctuations which we would describe in terms of two poles – *impotence* and *omnipotence*. It may be enhanced by a supporting destiny or diminished if it is employed in ways contrary to the destiny of the individual. Thus a young man may by dint of his industry, in keeping with his destiny, become a successful member of his community and so acquire more power, manifest, this time, in terms of economic, social or political advance. Chinua Achebe in his novel, *Things Fall Apart*, tells of the young Okwonkwo who by hard work became a successful farmer, thereby acquiring wealth and so able to take Ibo titles. Okwonkwo rose to prominence because he had been working along lines approved by his destiny (*chi*). He had risen 'from great poverty and misfortune to be one of the lords of the clan'.[14] His success however upset his attitude to his fellow-men and to the gods of the land. First, he became brusque to less successful men and on one occasion, he referred to one of his co-villagers, one Osugo by name, as woman, because the latter had contradicted him at a meeting of elders convened to determine the date of the next ancestral feast.[15] Next, he beat his wife during the Week of Peace heedless of the intervention of his friends and fellow-elders. Of course, he did give the local priest of the earth-goddess the obligatory placatory offering of one she-goat, one hen, a length of cloth and a hundred cowries; but he had by then made for himself enemies who had come to regard him as 'the little bird *nza*' whose fortunes has made him forget himself.[16] Again, to crown it all, his gun went off accidentally and killed the son of the old man Ezeudu, whose funeral rite was being celebrated. Okwonkwo had this time committed a mortal sin, indeed a serious crime against the earth-goddess; he had to flee to his mother's kinsmen; his house was burnt down and his homestead destroyed. He had transgressed the social codes of his village and naturally, violated the refinements of his destiny. So he went into voluntary exile to live with his mother's kin. There, although he was given a plot of land to cultivate, 'work no longer had for him the pleasure it used to have, and when there was no work to do he sat in a silent half-sleep'.[17] He who had once been one of the lords of his homeland had, as it were in a flash, become a castaway, a social and political nonentity. He was now an unimportant member of a strange community. His omnipotence had been reduced to impotence.

By the end of his exile, which had lasted seven years, Okwonkwo had once more recovered his omnipotence. He returned home in good spirits and resumed his former position in his village. He was once more a man to be reckoned with. Back home, he was hurt by the presence of Christian missionaries who had come to the village during his absence. So he fired a resistance to their activities; the villagers destroyed the church which had been built. Okwonkwo and five others were subsequently arrested but released on payment of a fine. On the day after their release, the six elders met their fellow villagers to report their sad experience. But the District Commissioner had sent five court messengers to deal with that situation. Okwonkwo challenged the leader but he stood his ground. In a flash, Okwonkwo decapitated him with his matchet. The meeting broke up in a tumult. Okwonkwo had displayed open resistance against Her Majesty's Government. In his despair, he hanged himself, perhaps to escape the District Commissioner's wrath. The cycle was at last complete. Okwonkwo had once more fallen from omnipotence to final impotence, without any hope of recovery in this life. He had taken his own life. He could not even be buried by his own kinsmen. Only 'strangers' were permitted to do so. His own people must however expiate the desecration.[18]

(B) COMMUNAL RELATIONSHIPS

The story of Okwonkwo illustrates the fact that however powerful or, for that matter, insignificant an African may be, he lives his life first, as a member of a community and next, as an individual. His family, his clan or his tribe comes first and himself as an individual, second. His activities may be personal but hardly individual. His whole life is always geared to the well-being of the community. So the various rites performed at the major crises of life-birth, adolesence, marriage and death – are communal. The following instances are illustrative:

(i) Birth
Sylvia Leith-Ross reports that among the Ibo, when a child is born, after the mother has come out of her seclusion, 'the child is named by three names, one given by the husband's family, one given by the mother's, one by the *dibia* (Medicine-man), who has been called in to divine what male or female ancestor has entered the child and names it accordingly'.[19]

In other words, both families cooperate in naming the child. Then they jointly celebrate a sacrificial feast, offering the blood of an animal victim – goat or fowl – to the ancestor. The parents, the newly-born and the ancestors are thus held together in one multifold community.

(ii) *Adolescence*

The adolescent (or perhaps adult) initiation rites provide an opportunity for the youth to understand that they had to live the life their fathers had lived before them, and their fathers before them.[20] They learn the lore of their land and are trained to serve their tribe or country in various ways, sometimes with life and limb. Only then are they free to marry and beget children. No young man is acceptable to the community who had not become identified with the ancestors through the initiation rites. To use the language of Levy Bruhl, 'The rites of initiation often seem to have as their essential aim to weld the new members of the clan definitely and finally into the mass of the ancestors'.[21] The initiate is now fully integrated into his clan or tribe by a simulated death and, then, a birth.

(iii) *Marriage*

Marriage is essentially a transaction between two families. Exogamous marriage, when complete, makes it socially acceptable that the bride goes off to live with her husband, thereby breaking herself away from her clan. Her children are born into their father's clan and she technically remains a stranger. But as in the case of the Shona, at a certain date after a wedding, the young couple return to the parents of the bride and eat their first meal together with the wife's parents. Gelfand reports that a ceremony, *masungiro*, is performed on that occasion, for which the couple take with them 'some goats or cattle'. The ceremony is of course 'considered of great importance as it is believed that if this ceremony is neglected sickness can befall the parents'.[22]

Among the Swazi, not only do 'maternal grandparents beg the father to send the child on visits', but the maternal kin must be kept informed of any illness. Very often, a woman and her children are said to be 'saved' by the 'ancestors of the maternal home'.[23] Any breach of the sex-regulations of the community leads to trouble. For example, as among the Mende of Sierra Leone, not only do the offenders fall ill, but when, say, a man and a woman practise sexual intercourse on arable land, the crops sown on it afterwards fail to yield good harvests.[24] The case of Okwonkwo already mentioned, beating his wife during the Week of Peace is indeed a good instance.[25] A third instance, consonant with the second, is the belief that when a man fails on a business mission, his wife must be guilty of adultery. The adultery may have been committed before he set off or in his absence.[26] Violations of the social regulations therefore cause the offender sickness, failure or disaster. The antidote is essentially provided by cultic rites.

One feature of this corporate relationship is the demand on the individual to maintain a mode of life which enhances the total well-being of the community. This demand is manifest in several ways. We mention two. First, the individual is said to be born with a destiny which he must fulfil during his life-time. The Yoruba refer to this notion as *Ori* the Ibo as *chi*, and the Akan as *nkrabea*. We would briefly observe here that the destiny is believed to come from God. The Yoruba believe that this destiny may be chosen by the individual or granted at his request; or it may be an affixture by Olodumare, the Supreme Being. According to the Akan, the newly born comes to the world with a mission. In both cases, one has a duty to fulfil one's destiny. Danquah states that when a person fails to fulfil his destiny, he must return to earth through a re-incarnation to accomplish the unfulfilled part of his mission. This fulfilment however demands a rapport between one's natural inclinations and one's *ori* or *kra*, or *chi*. Otherwise life would be a failure; Okwonkwo's *chi* had said 'nay' to his ambitions. The Akan indeed stress that if one's life was perverse thereby deviating from the *nkrabea*, at death one is not allowed to be re-incarnated until he had gained the pardon of the reigning king.[27] Among the Mende, the destiny of the individual, *nɛmi*, it is believed, depends for its realisation upon his relationship with his fellow-men. Every word of blessing (i.e. good wish) increases the fructification of the destiny.[28] One could therefore infer that bad relationships with those among whom an individual lives would deter the realisation of his destiny.

Second, the well-being of the community is explicitly understood as being maintained and preserved by various cultic demands and taboos. Violations of these demands bring about illnesses of one form or another.

3. SOCIO – RELIGIOUS AND EMOTIONAL PRESSURES:

We may now assemble some of the emotional needs of the tribal African which call for relief – we would say, salvation. We mention four, three of them collective and one personal.

119

First, the anxiety which originates from the day to day problems of life. For example, the inconsistences of the weather, the hazards of everyday life in encounters with wild beast and poisonous snakes; the high rate of infantile mortality; the desire for children, especially sons.

Second, the anxiety which is born of the fear of evil spirits and malicious persons, witches and sorcerers.

These two forms of anxiety may be removed by religious rites designed to that end.

Third, the concern for good relationships with the ancestral spirits as well as with the cultic spirits they worship. Here too, appropriate rites have been developed both to keep the ancestors happy and well-disposed to their descendants, and to maintain rapport with the cultic spirits.

These three areas are related to the well-being of the individual but, in fact, directly affect the well-being of the community, be it the family, the clan or the tribe. Busia has recorded for us a prayer to the royal ancestors at the *Odwera* ceremony – an annual festival of the Akan, which illustrates this dual relationship:

'Here is food; all you ancestors receive this and eat; the year has come round again; today we celebrate it; bring us blessing; blessing to the chief who sits on your stool; health to the people; let women bear children; let the men prosper in their undertakings; life to all; we thank you for the good harvest; for standing behind us well (i.e. guarding and protecting us); Blessing, blessing, blessing'.[29]

The clue to this prayer and others like it is *Power* – vital-power which subsists in the Supreme Being, man, and the non-human spirits.[30]

Fourth, the desire to maintain this vital-power at its best. To achieve this desire, various rites are performed which are designed to cleanse the tribe, the clan, the family and the individual. The experience of rising from *impotence* to *omnipotence* represents the cultivation of this *power* from nothingness to the zenith of its potentiality; whilst the fall from omnipotence to impotence represents its deterioration and final decadence at death. Its maintenance or development depends upon purificatory rites by which the spirits are propitiated and the community is cleansed. Okwonkwo had to offer a she-goat, a hen, a length of cloth and a hundred cowries to the priest of Ana, the earth-goddess, to propitiate the offended deity for beating his wife during the holy Week of Peace; his house was burnt down and his homestead destroyed to purify the village from the curse of having killed the son of the deceased elder whose funeral rites were being celebrated; he himself had to go into exile for seven years to remove the pollution of his person from the village.

Mende men and women who violate the sex taboos have to be ritually cleansed and purified to enable them to retain their respective place in the community.[31] The *Odwera* ceremony also affords the Akan an opportunity for 'cleansing the tribe from defilement, and for the purification of the shrines'. Busia tells us that 'The chief took a ritual bath and water was sprinkled on the shrines and all who were present, as a symbolic act of cleansing'.[32]

It is therefore reasonable to suggest that when all is well, the people may be said to be collectively strong and pure and therefore light. Otherwise, the community through its individuals are weighed down by frustration, despair, disappointment, failure, sickness and ultimately death. Since the source of evil is externalized, and therefore personalized, cases of disappointments, frustrations, sickness and even death, especially of young children are attributed to what Monica Wilson describes as *potency*, e.g. witchcraft and sorcery (and theft), on the one hand, and on the other, menstruation, recent sex-activity, masturbation especially when practised by a girl.[33] Witchcraft, sorcery and theft are of course anti-social and destroy life or the hopes of others thereby creating an instability of one form or another in the community. The victim is affected by the deeds of others than himself. Masturbation, recent sex-activity or menstruation, on the other hand, are personal to the individuals concerned. And yet, the community is equally affected adversely in both cases. The one, destroying the communal life by an act planned and directed against someone else, the other, generating in the person or persons concerned a danger-radiating influence. So to be saved from both forms of *potency*, *protective* rites are performed which immunise potential victims from witches, sorcerers, thieves and evil spirits, on the one hand, and, on the other, *purificatory* rites which remove the danger-radiating pollution which would ordinarily destroy the person of the individual concerned. The ancestral rites seem to fulfil both functions. The ancestors are both appeased in case they were offended and petitioned to support as well as protect their descendants.

4. THE CONCEPT OF GUILT IN INDIGENOUS AFRICAN CULTURE

From the preceding discussion it would have become clear that, to use the Akan as a model, it is the personality–soul of man which needs to be 'saved'. The life-soul always is pure although its vital-power may be decreased by any damage done by *potency* to the personality-soul.[34] Hence as it has been already noted Williamson

121

states that 'as to man and his needs, the Akan interprets this, not in terms of sin but in vitalistic terms'. Or again, the Akan knows 'no problem of sin' or 'problem of suffering'. J.V. Taylor, followed by F.B. Welbourn, says that the African world-view belongs to a 'shame culture' rather than to a 'guilt culture'.[35] At the Seventh Seminar held at the University of Ghana in 1965 on Christianity in Tropical Africa, Father Mulago criticised Welbourn's denial to Africans of 'a sense of guilt.' Other participants of the conference had similar views.[36] We would say that the guilt-factor does in fact play an important role in African tribal society. Okwonkwo, already referred to, is a good example of a man adjudged guilty by the Priest of Ana, his co-villagers and himself. He left his home during the same night in which he killed the young boy, albeit accidentally. The Rev. Alexander Hetherwick is therefore not convincing when he postulates a 'lack of a sense of crime and the punishment of it as an offence against society or the State . . .'[37] A young Sierra Leonean who recently underwent a female adult initiation rite could not stop bleeding after the ritual operation until, urged by a diviner, she had confessed to a theft some time prior to the ceremony. The question therefore arises as to what the point of reference of the guilt, so posited, may be. Perhaps we might take a lead from the Lugbara and say that such acts as destroy the stability of the community,[38] be it the family or the authority of the tribal rulers or the moral sanctions of the ancestors or the tutelary deities, constitute sin among tribal Africans and become the ground of guilt.

Anyone so convicted – sometimes by himself – therefore has to undergo a rite of cleansing to restore his sense of well-being, both moral and spiritual. Sometimes as in the case of witches, the cleansing may be followed by a *protective* rite. One can therefore understand why in the religious life of the African, priestcraft and sacrifice are so important. The sacrificial rites demand and help to preserve clan or community fellowship; they also ensure its future maintenance. Thus the crucial necessity for restoring a 'cool heart' among the ancestors or maintaining good relationships with the tutelary deities, to take two examples, is an index of a deep-seated inward effect of the rites on the offerers.

There is however a further element which must be considered, viz whether or not the salvation attained in respect of the personality–soul is thought by tribal Africans to affect the whole man. This is an important consideration for Christians who seek to pass on to tribal Africans their concepts of sin, salvation and judgment. Since, to recapitulate, to the African, sin is 'destruction of the stability of the community', and therefore to defraud one's neighbour, to cause a little child anguish, to place a piece of lighted charcoal into the hands of a blind man begging for gifts, or to have sex-intercourse on arable land, is to destroy the stability of the community, and therefore sinful; since also the purificatory or placatory rites only affect the personality-soul, and further, since it is believed the personality-soul remains on earth, in the land of shadows, how is the Christian understanding of God's judgment on the soul to be interpreted to tribal Africans? Moreover, since in the African context, judging from Danquah's position, the life-soul which returned to the Supreme Being under judgment is indeed always pure and has no taint of evil, it must be agreed that the Christian teaching on salvation does not easily fit into the tribal African concept of salvation.

5. CONCLUSION

Life for the tribal African consists of situations, sometimes unpre-dictable, but at other times consequential to his role as a member of a community, which demand of him certain modes of conduct which are consonant with the promotion of the well-being of the community in general. But although his general interests are subsumed by those which relate to the enhancement of his family or clan or the tribe, his real contribution to the community depends on his personal well-being.

This is a spiritual condition although it is made manifest in the physical and economic well-being of the individuals concerned. Therefore, the well-being of the community as such is a reflection of the morality of the individuals who constitute it. So thieves, witches and sorcerers are regarded as anti-social and therefore destructive forces which endanger the life of the community; menstruation, recent sex acts and masturbation all release in or through the persons involved, dangerous energies which militate against the normal working structure of the family and the community at large. Resort to healing at both the moral and physical levels therefore becomes the natural means of restoring the vitality of the community. The spiritual forces which are inhibitory to progress must be removed. So purificatory rites feature in many instances; other rites designed to remove the dangers attributable to witches or sorcerers are of course primarily protective. The purificatory, and more so the propitiatory rites demand confession and absolution. The frustrations which generally follow therefore have an inward meaning to those involved. It is significant that in the Musama Disco Christo Church, described by Baeta as 'the largest and most highly-organised of the indigenous "spiritual churches" in Ghana',[39] emphasis is laid at their healing session on the spiritual preparation of the patients. The patients 'prepare themselves for the healing service by holding the prescribed fast and upon the day of the service, ceremonially washing themselves'; 'they must wash meticulously all the orifices of their body, and their armpits'.[40] This preparation is in consonant with the belief that witches leave their bodies at night through the nine orifices.

The Christian Church may yet have to discover ways of interpreting the tribal purificatory rites so that African converts to Christianity may learn to refer their effects to the life-soul of the individual. Soteriology in the African situation must therefore not be thought of purely in terms of Christ's death but more so in terms of his priestly act which may be summarised in the words of the Fourth Evangelist:

'for their sake I now consecrate myself, that they too may be consecrated by the truth'. (John 17:19).

The consecration of the Christian however refers to the life-soul which is subject to the judgment of God.

The search must go on.

CHRISTIAN EVANGELISTIC STRATEGY IN WEST AFRICA

Reflections on the Centenary of the Consecration of Bishop Samuel Adjayi Crowther on St Peter's Day, 1864

A hundred years ago, on St Peter's Day, 1864, Adjayi Crowther was consecrated Bishop of the Niger, and his first major assignment was to answer the call of King William Pepple, the King of Bonny, to establish a Christian mission in his town and the surrounding district. While not forgetting Crowther's earlier missionary exploits in Nigeria, we wish here to consider his work in the Niger Delta Pastorate, and so to try to discover some of the principles which guided his thinking and his work.

Bishop Crowther's achievements, as is well known, were quite revolutionary in his day. We, a hundred years afterwards, have the privilege of inheriting the fruit of his labours. But we must now seek to make a new thrust in the propagation of the Gospel in this century in order to redeem the best elements of African traditional life and take them up to Christ.

Crowther's father was a man of royal descent, who maintained a coterie of idols. But when the Ifa oracle was consulted at Crowther's birth, he was declared an ɔmɔ-ɔlɔrun (more accurately known as *Aluja*); that is to say, he was to be a votary of ɔlɔrun, not of any *orisha*.[1] Had God in His divine wisdom separated the boy Adjayi from birth to reveal Jesus Christ to him? Certainly, after various misadventures as a slave-boy, he was set free in Sierra Leone, taught to read and write, and baptised Samuel Crowther. In 1864 he became the first African Anglican bishop, and proved to be the St Paul of West African Christianity. From 1864 until his death on December 31, 1891, he sought to promote the Christian faith in Nigeria. In a charge delivered at Lokoja on September 13, 1869, he remarked that

Christianity has come into the world to abolish and supersede all false religions, to direct mankind to the only way of obtaining peace and reconciliation with their offended God. It condemns all

125

vices, reforms the morals, and recommends virtues as laid down in the Gospel by Christ. . . . These we must impress upon the minds of our converts from heathenism, and point out to them from the Word of God.

But it should be borne in mind that Christianity does not undertake to destroy national assimilation: where there are many degrading and superstitious defects it corrects them; where they are connected with politics, such corrections should be introduced with due caution, and with all meekness of wisdom, that there may be good and perfect understanding between us and the powers that be, that while we render to all their dues, we may regard it as our bounden duty to stand firm in rendering to God the things which are God's.

Crowther could say the same to-day with equal relevance to the new, rapidly developing situation in West Africa.

The charge goes on:

Their native mutual-aid clubs should not be despised, but where there is any connexion with superstitions, they should be corrected and improved [note the words] after a Christian model. Amusements are acknowledged on all hands to tend to relieve the mind and sharpen the intellect. If any such is not immoral or indecent, tending to corrupt the mind, but merely an innocent play for amusement, it should not be checked because of its being native and of a heathen origin. Often this kind of amusement are fables, story-telling, proverbs and songs, which may be regarded as stores of their national education in which the heathen exercise their power of thinking: such will be improved upon and enriched from foreign stocks as civilization advances. Their religious terms and ceremonies should be carefully noticed: a wrong use made of such terms does not depreciate their real value, but renders them more valuable when we adopt them in expressing Scriptural terms in their right senses and places, though they may have been misapplied.[2]

I have quoted this charge in extenso because I believe we are now at a point where, more than ever, the Christian Church in West Africa has to grapple with the problems Crowther enunciated and to find an answer soon. Let me summarise the problem. We in West Africa have postulated ancestral and other spirits and myriads of divinities, in the quest for concrete manifestations of divine authority. These postulates are human creations, designed to satisfy

126

our human emotional longings. As I see it, these longings can best be satisfied by Christianity, but Protestant Christianity unfortunately does not seem to be adequately equipped to meet this need. The increasing call by educated African nationalists, some of whom were once Christian, for a return to the 'old gods' means that devout Christians must be alert and circumspect, if the pagan deities are not to supersede Christianity. Crowther's work in the Niger Delta provides a useful guide to the strategy required for our present needs.

The situation in Brass is an instance. Here an ivory god was revered; ivory installed in a grove had assumed numinous qualities. More devastating was the snake *ju-ju*, a boa constrictor. Here was a land infested with boa constrictors, which moved around freely, taking up chickens and other domestic animals and sometimes entering a house and picking up babies who had been left alone. No one dared to kill them. If anyone did, he made restitution to the priest: ten pounds if he was a master; a slave had to give his life. If a boa constrictor died in a fire, the owner of the house was held responsible and must pay ten pounds or the value of a slave. If he had nothing with which to pay, he had to give one of his relatives to the chief priest as a slave.[3] The corollary of this belief was that any creeper came to be regarded as a member of the reptile family and had to be preserved. Cultivation of the land was prohibited, except on a limited scale, and no yams could be grown. To cultivate the land was to cut down creepers; to grow yams would lead inevitably to the cutting and killing of the vine after the crops had been harvested. The *ju-ju* was centred on a chief priest, who imposed penalties for its infringement.

A different situation was found in Bonny. Here the *ju-ju* was located in a sacred grove which the layman must not enter. Only the priests had access to the grove. Bishop Crowther, either by accident or by intuition, requested the use of this place for the erection of a mission station. When the grove was cleared, it was found to contain immolated bodies and the skeletons of twins which had been thrown there alive, to die. The Bishop's methods are quite instructive. He said, 'Give us the ground and leave us and the *ju-ju* to settle the remaining palaver'.[4] He had the courage to assert that God was superior to the spirits. So he encouraged the Christian Prince George Pepple (after a reading of Holy Scripture) to clear the sacred grove. A chief, Banigo by name, was encouraged by this action to clear a large plot of ground close to the projected mission station, and he cultivated it with good results 'to the surprise of all'.[5] After the grove had been cleared, the Bishop arranged for twin babies to be looked after by the mission station. The pagan priests objected, but this objection was later overcome and the proposal was accepted. Later still, through the example of the wife of an influential chief, twins were no longer removed from their normal surroundings. Indeed, it is reported that from that time onwards, women began to pray 'to be blessed with twins'.[6]

Similarly, we recall with joy that the snake *ju-ju* at Brass ended when King Ockiya and some of his chiefs who were favourably disposed towards Christianity cleared the jungle, cut down all creepers, planted yams and reaped a bumper harvest. We take pride in the knowledge that on Easter Day, April 21, 1867, King George Pepple decreed the iguana *ju-ju* violate, and iguanas were no longer sacrosanct.[7] But it seems to me that now, a hundred years after the penetration of Christianity into Nigeria, we ought to ask ourselves whether it has taken deep root in West Africa. In particular, we need to consider whether we could produce a distinctively African liturgy – sufficiently African to be a reflection of our society and, at the same time, sufficiently Christian to fit naturally into the system of world Christianity. To my mind, any effective liturgy should express:

(i) *A concept of Deity*. Is God all-terrible, awesome and unapproachable? Or is He a God of love, merciful, long-suffering and forgiving? Is He a king, all-sovereign, or one of a body of coequal divinities, *primus inter pares*? Is He a Father who cares for the well-being of mankind and loves them unreservedly? Is He far from human reach, or have we ready access to Him? Is He the Creator and Provider of the universe?

(ii) *A doctrine of man*. Are we God's children, even by adoption, or are we His slaves? Or are we both, like 'the son who serves his father'? Many of our people talk of God as our great Ancestor – *Ɔlɔrun* or *Olodumare*, *Ɔnyame* or *Nyankopon*. What do they mean?

At the same time, man asserts his freedom of action, which tends to make him resist the demands of the society in which he lives and, in particular, resist the will of God. In Africa this attitude is seen both in the postulation of minor deities and in the violation of cultic sanctions. A liturgy, then, should include a statement of man's relation to God and should also express:

(iii) *A doctrine of sin and salvation*. Here the operative elements in the African situation are illness and a breach with the community, which call for confession, absolution, the offer of sacrifice as expiation, and restoration to society. These acts require a priest who offers sacrifice.

There is an instructive entry in Crowther's journals relating to a god, Abara, who eats new yams: 'Abara will absolve them [the people of Bonny] of their sins, but if they were to eat the new yam first, without honouring the Abara, he would kill them'. So the people offer gifts of yams to Abara and wait to be 'baptized' by the high priest, who receives 'gifts of rum, gin and manillas'.[8] This is not a peculiar phenomenon: it represents a situation very common in West Africa; namely, the god, the priest and the sacrifice. In the sacrificial system of the Ibos, Crowther saw a spring-board for teaching about the sacrifice of Christ. Of particular importance for us here is the fact that the piacular rites used in African cults provide a way of restoration to health and society for those who have fallen ill because they have violated certain sanctions. Illness and bad spirituality (we would say 'sin') are correlates in Africa. So the patient must pay a votive offering to the god he feels he has offended. The total act includes a confession of sin, a sacrifice, an absolution and a ritual, after which the patient returns home either feeling completely well or confident of a speedy recovery. Moreover, since worship is so intimately connected with the well-being of society, the violation of any religious sanction leads to alienation from society; but once the deity has been propitiated, the patient is restored to his group as a regular member of it.

If Christianity is to penetrate West Africa, it must foster an appreciation of true penitence and, at the same time, include the possibility of spiritual healing through the offer of forgiveness granted by the rite of absolution. The so-called 'spiritual churches' include provisions of this nature for their members.[9] In this respect, Crowther's advice at Lokoja deserves serious consideration: 'Christianity does not undertake to destroy national assimilation: where there are many degrading and superstitious defects it corrects them.' We should therefore look into the piacular rites and seek to correct the superstitious elements in them by offering our congregations the means to spiritual and emotional equilibrium. These means are provided by confession and absolution.

This assimilation of native tradition also extends to the family, particularly to family solidarity between the living and the dead, which we Africans are still able to maintain. Of course, our pagan prayers are primarily petitions to the dead for the main necessities of life,[10] although some could be classed as intercessions. They assume that the ancestral spirits are capable of self-determination and of responding to requests put to them. As Christians, our petitions will be for all men, in their several callings. But we have also to consider the question of prayers for the dead, especially in our liturgy. Do we feel differently towards our ancestral dead from non-Christians? Or do we live two lives – the one Christian, which has little, if any, concern for our dead; the other, when we shed Christianity and become Africans again, as in the case of the Yoruba *Egungun* cult? This is a psychological state of paranoia, of split personality. While often referring to the 'two natures' of Christ (as perfect God and perfect man), the doctrine of the Incarnation stresses the *oneness* of the personality. Any future liturgy for Africans, therefore, must cater for the various aspects of our life; and we must pay attention to the problem of prayers for the dead on the one hand, and of intercessions by the dead on our behalf on the other.

In practice, Christianity has always recognised these in respect of the faithful. But the solidarity of the Christian family compels us to ask whether the unconverted, unbaptised dead share in the benefits of Christian conversion after their death. Is 'conversion by osmosis' possible? Is not osmosis inherent in the Christian concept of the family? For example, St Paul regards the marriage of a Christian to a non-Christian as 'holy' (I Cor. 7:14, 16) – at least, the children are holy. The individual members of the family benefit from the group, in terms of ideas, plans or social connexions. In Christian terms, we would add grace and covenant to this list. The covenant aspect is fundamental to the Christian life, and is vital in any discussion of the place of the departed and their rôle in the Church. But to revert to osmosis: was not this the principle behind the preservation of vines and creepers and the prohibition against the planting of yams at Brass in Crowther's time? Every vine and creeper behaves like a snake, so if the snake becomes sacrosanct, so do all creepers. Again, when a plot of ground is set apart as a sacred grove, its environs become sacred and cannot be cleared for cultivation. The Ɛbɔ ɛtutu of the Yoruba is another good example of osmosis.[11] In the belief that an illness or disability is transferred, the victim is laid under an *iroko* tree and it is assumed that the first person who passes by will attract the illness or disability to himself.

Another factor is the relationship between ourselves and our departed ancestors, particularly those who never heard of Jesus Christ. Crowther was aware of this problem and asked in 1869, 'What shall become of the heathen who die without having the opportunity of hearing the Gospel of Jesus Christ?' After referring to *Romans* 1:14, he went on to say, 'With all submission, I will remark that it is not the will of God to reveal unto us what shall become of such persons'. Later, he offered a solution in the following words:

Thou who knowest thy master's will, but doest it not, shalt be beaten with many stripes, in proportion to your light, knowledge

130

and opportunity you have, but which you have abused. The heathens who have not the like opportunity of knowing, but commit things worthy of stripes, shall be beaten with few stripes, in proportion to their lack of additional knowledge and light.[12]

Now, a hundred years later, we must go further, in view of the persistence of initiation ceremonies and ancestral cults. Let me state the problem in a new way: are we in danger of creating the impression that Christianity breaks into the social solidarity of the African and that we Christians may find ourselves in a 'Christian' heaven from which those for whom we have great personal affection are excluded?[13] Of course, we must pray for the faithful departed – for Samuel Crowther, John Christopher Taylor, King William Pepple, King Ockiya and the many Christian missionaries and converts of the Niger Expeditions. But what of their relatives and friends? This question is a fundamental one, because it raises the issues of survival after death and of conversion to Christianity in the state of survival. The answer to these questions must be sought in two further doctrines which should be expressed in an African liturgy, namely:

(iv) *a doctrine of the Incarnation*;

(v) *a doctrine of the Church*.

An understanding of the Christian doctrine of the Incarnation is the answer to human groping after God – *Orunmila*, *Oduduwa*, the *orishas* of Yorubaland, the snake and ivory *ju-jus* in Brass, the iguana *ju-ju* at Bonny and the many other cults all over West Africa. Christians believe that God manifested Himself in the human form of His Son, who is the image of the invisible God, the first-born of all creation and the first-born from the dead; by Him all things were created and in Him all things hang together. He is the head of the Church, the first-born of many brethren. By His death He overcame death. Indeed, the language of 1 *Peter* 3:18 points to the extension of the influence of Christ's death to the unregenerate dead. In strict theological language this is a myth; but it represents a great truth and expresses the deep longings of the early Church. The early Christians were undoubtedly concerned about the fate of their relatives who were not privileged to be alive when the Christ was born. But they were equally sure that Jesus had become the centre of a new family, the Church. This is the great family of God, of which Jesus Christ is the first-born (Rom. 8:29). But Jesus Christ was the *universal* during His incarnate life; and if the writer of *Ephesians* is right in saying that God had purposed from before the foundation of ther world to 'sum up all things in Christ', then the myth of 1 *Peter* 3:18 is in keeping with the doctrine of Christ's lordship over all things.

131

In Africa the family is of supreme significance. We make a covenant with our dead and thereby maintain an active covenant relationship among the living.[14] Indeed, we regard the ancestors as co-guardians of the mores of our communities. Thus, two Yoruba who have a dispute may go to the grave of an ancestor where each asserts his innocence of the charge, on the ground that the ancestors are in a position to determine the truth. Then they take an oath, each saying something like this: 'May I die in seven days if I have made a false statement'.[15] The Creoles always refer to the ancestors as those who are now capable of apprehending the truth and address them as 'you who now live in the world of truth'. Naturally, the ancestors do not hear or respond. Our belief in their power is based on specific psychological reactions which we have learned to cultivate.[16] Should Christians decry this attitude uncritically? I would suggest not. Of course, we must strive to correct those aspects of this belief which are contrary to the Christian faith. We must help the worshippers to discover something significant in native religious practices which will lead to more acceptable activities than the mere maintenance of virtuosity, as in the case of the Kalabari *Owu* dancers or the *Egungun* mimics of Yorubaland.

This brings us finally to the question: how far can we devise a thoroughly African liturgy? Professor Idowu would say that we should exclude from it anything which savours of European origins.[17] This, I humbly submit, is too radical a point of view. The advanced technology which we study and practise in Africa is not of African origin. There is no good reason why the Christian Church should not draw on the deposit of Christian thinking and practice throughout the ages. In any case, Serapion's Prayer Book has come down to us from Egypt. But we have also to be alive to the needs of the current situation. For instance, when the Prime Minister of Sierra Leone, Sir Milton Margai, died last year, a ceremony was arranged to mark the fortieth day after his death, in which provision was made both for a traditional native celebration and also for Christian services, specially compiled for the occasion. I think that Christians in Sierra Leone were right to take part in the events, as Christians. Here is a clear instance of the Church's assimilation, however indirect, of an African practice. The Church in West Africa should provide for other similar contingencies by taking into account the present needs of its members.

In respect of the African attitude to the ancestral dead, particularly to the heroes of the land, this could be done by producing a Calendar of West African Saints, with Samuel Adjayi Crowther first on the list. Why should the Church not declare December 31 a black-letter

132

day, on which the Province of West Africa should hold commemorative services to thank God for the life and ministry of this great missionary? Each constituent diocese could then prepare a further list of names for commemoration. This would be in keeping with the thinking of the 1958 Lambeth Conference expressed in the preparatory document, *The Commemoration of Saints and Heroes of the Faith in the Anglican Communion*. In pagan Africa, local heroes have always received special consideration, *pace* Edward Blyden,[18] and this is true for various tribes in West Africa.

If the Church is to make a real impact in West Africa, its doctrine of God must be restated to stress His universal fatherhood and to provide a Christian counterpart of the pagan concept of God as our ancestor. This will naturally require fresh consideration of the doctrines of man, of sin and salvation, and of the Church, in the light of the Incarnation of Jesus Christ who, as man, sought to align His will perfectly with the will of God. It must be emphasised that in Jesus Christ man has access to God in a way that is not possible through the Yoruba *orishas* or through any of the deities which abound in West African cosmology. The teaching of Jesus that spiritual health and salvation can come only through complete surrender to the will of God as manifested in Him must also be included. This new relationship is based on the New Covenant, ratified in Christ's blood when He offered Himself on the Cross as the one, perfect Offering.

All this means that Christians must realise (a) that the essence of pagan worship is sacramental[19] and (b) that therefore only Christian sacramental worship centred on a sacrificing priest and worshippers seeking spiritual and physical restoration can provide a true substitute for pagan forms.

In this connexion, I should like to add in closing that at the celebrations in Lagos marking the centenary of Bishop Crowther's consecration, the Church of the Province of West Africa lost a great opportunity when, at the special service held round his grave in the Ajele Cemetery on June 28, 1964, no prayers were said for him. A requiem mass would have been most apt. Pagan Yoruba would undoubtedly have recognised the presence of a hero-ancestor whose grave they visited and would have addressed a few words to him. We Christians did not think it necessary to pray on behalf of the greatest African missionary.

'Rest eternal grant unto Samuel Adjayi Crowther, O Lord,
May light perpetual shine upon him.'

133

NOTES

THE PRACTICE OF PRESENCE (PAGES 1–10)

1. John Baillie, *The Sense of the Presence of God*, London 1962, p. 33.
2. E.O. James, *Religion and Reality*, London 1950, p. 10. Vincent Vycinas, *Earth and Gods*, the Hague, 1961, pp. 29, 216–220.
3. Ruth Finegan, *Limba Stories*, London 1967, Story of *Adama and Ifu*, pp. 67ff.
4. R.S. Rattray, *Ashanti*, Oxford 1923, p. 258–262f.
5. Daryll Forde, *African Worlds*, London 1954, essay by K.A. Busia on *The Ashanti*, p. 195. cp Kenneth Little, *The Mende of Sierra Leone*, London 1951, p. 225.
6. Hans Abrahamsson, *The Origin of Death*, (Studia Ethnographia Uppsaliensia III E.T.) London 1951, p. 73.
7. C.F. Schlenker, *A Collection of Temne Traditions, Fables etc.* London 1864, p. 28f.
8. Rattray, *Ashanti*, Oxford 1923, p. 54.
9. cp Fr Placide Tempels, *Bantu Philosophy*, Presence Africaine 1959, pp. 30–39, 64f.
10. Lucien Levy-Bruhl, *The 'Soul' of the Primitive* E.T. London 1965, p. 19; cp Ernst Cassirer, *The Philosophy of Symbolic Forms*, New Haven 1960 Edition, Vol. II, pp. 156, 179, 183.
11. Rudolf Otto, *The Idea of the Holy*, London 1931, cap 3, 4.
12. John MacMurray, *The Self as Agent*, London 1957, p.117.
13. cp Ernst Cassirer, *op. cit.*, p. 168f.
14. cp E.B. Idowu, *Olodumare*, London 1962 Cap 13; *Odu*, No. 2 Article by Bradbury on *Ehi*; Meyer Fortes, *Oedipus and Job*, Cambridge 1959, Cap 61.
15. Eva Meyerowitz, *The Akan of Ghana*, pp. 47, 146. H. Debrunner, *Witchcraft in Ghana*, Kumasi 1959, Cap 3. Dr. J.B. Danquah refers to the *kra* as the soul, and to the *sunsum* as personality. (*The Akan Doctrine of God*, London 1944 Section IV, Cap. II, p. 111f); Meyer Fortes, *Oedipus and Job*.

16. This notion is present in the attitude towards rain as the divine seminal fluid which fertilises the Earth. (cp Ernst Cassirer, *op. cit.,* p. 190).
17. Ernst Cassirer, *op. cit.,* p. 192.
18. C.F. Schlenker, *op. cit.,* p. 13ff.
19. A. Radcliffe-Brown and Daryll Forde, *African Systems of Kinship and Marriage,* London 1962, p. 72; cp J.H. Middleton, *Lugbara Religion,* London 1960, p. 111.
20. B.J.F. Lanbscher, *Sex, Custom and Psycho-Pathology,* London 1951, p. 51.
21. *ibidem,* p. 8f.
22. *ibidem,* p. 13f.
23. Alistair Scobie, *Murder for Magic,* London 1965.
24. Chief Anthony Enahorto, *Fugitive Offender,* London 1965, p. 25f; Malinowski, for example, says that witchcraft is on the increase with the expansion of European civilisations (see *The Dynamics of Culture Change,* New Haven and London, 1945, p. 94).
25. See the remark of C.G. Baeta of Ghana 'our people live with their dead' (*Christianity and African Culture,* Accra 1955 p. 591); cp. Ernst Cassirer *op. cit.* p. 175f.
26. cp *Sierra Leone Bulletin of Religion,* Vol. 7, No. 2, December 1965, pp. 48–55. Article by Harry Sawyerr on *Some Graveside Libations in and near Freetown.*
27. I.T. Ramsey, *Religious Language,* London 1957, p. 47, see the whole of Cap. 1.
28. See E.B. Idowu, *op. cit.,* pp. 55, 67f. Samuel Johnson, *A History of the Yorubas,* London 1921, p. 38.
29. cp. K.A. Busia in Daryll Forde, *op. cit.,* p. 191–3.

THE DOGMA OF SUPER-SIZE (PAGES 11–25)

1. Hans Abrahamsson, *The Origin of Death* (Studia Ethnographia Uppsaliensia, III (English Edition), London, 1951, p. 73.
2. cp. Vincent Taylor, *The Gospel according to St. Mark,* London, 1955, p. 186, on Mark 1. 40; E.W.G. Masterman in J. Hastings, *Dictionary of Christ and the Gospels,* Edinburth, 1906, vol. II, p. 24–26.
3. Mircea Eliade, *Patterns of Comparative Religion* (E.T.), London, 1958, p. 27.
4. E. Evans Pritchard, 'Witchcraft' in *Africa,* VIII, 1935.
5. E.B. Idowu, *Olodumare,* London, 1962, p. 19 and footnote.
6. R.T. Parsons in E.W. Smith, *African Ideas of God,* London, 1950, p. 278.
7. cp. Mircea Eliade, *op. cit.,* p. 14.
8. cp. Harry Sawyerr, 'Sacrificial Rituals in Sierra Leone', *Sierra Leone Bulletin of Religion,* i, 1959, p. 14.
9. C. Northcote Thomas, *Law and Custom of the Timne and other Tribes,* London, 1916, p. 76; cp. P. Amaury Talbot, *Some Nigerian Fertility Cults,* London, 1927, p. 33f., 124.

10. C. Northcote Thomas, *op. cit.*, p. 76.
11. *ibid.*, p. 115.
12. *ibid.*, p. 76.
13. J. Wilson-Haffenden, *The Red men of Nigeria*, London, 1930, p. 176.
14. R.C. Rattray, *Ashanti*, London, 1926, p. 263.
15. Margaret J. Field, *Search for Security*, London, 1960, p. 41; Eva Meyerowitz, *The Sacred State of the Akan*, London, 1961, p. 199.
16. P. Amaury Talbot remarks that among the Ibo a husband is not permitted to try to view his wife's genitals. Violation of this privilege is regarded as grounds for a divorce. (*op. cit.*, p. 33f.).
17. Mircea Eliade, *The Myth of the Eternal Return* (E.T.), New York, 1954, p. 4.
18. C. Gustav Jung, *Psychological Types* (E.T.), London, 1923, p. 601.
19. Raymond Firth, *Man and Culture*, London 1957, p. 197, Essay on *Malinowski on Magic and Religion* by S.F. Nadel.
20. Nnamde Azikwe, *Renascent Africa*, Accra 1937, p. 145.
21. *ibid.*
22. See Ulli Beier, *Die Religion der Yoruba in West-Nigeria*, in Kumba Tam, Darmstadt, 1957, quoted by Jahnheinz Jahn in *Muntu*, London, 1961, p. 63 and footnote; The history of *Shango* is particularly suggestive; see E. Bolaji Idowu, *Olodumare*, London 1962, pp. 89–94.
23. Eva Meyerowitz, *The Divine Kingship in Ghana and Ancient Egypt*, London 1960, p. 27f.; *The Akan of Ghana*, London 1958, p. 24f.
24. J.T. Alldridge, *The Sherbro and Its Hinterland*, London 1901, p. 148.
25. Sidney de la Rue, *The Land of the Pepper Bird, Liberia*, New York 1930, p. 128.
26. cp. C. Ogden and I.A. Richards, *The Meaning of Meaning*, London 1936, p. 320f.
27. Mircea Eliade, *Patterns in Comparative Religion*, London 1958, p. 13.
28. Ruth Benedict, Article on Myth in *Encyclopaedia of the Social Sciences*, London and New York 1949, Vol. II, Part I.
29. *Journal of American Folklore* Vol. 68, 1955, Article on the *Structural Study of Myth* by Claude P. Levi Strauss.
30. Nnamdi Azikwe, *op. cit.* p. 143.
31. *ibid.*
32. *ibid.*
33. The Masked dancers who are usually performing in the town have to find some secluded spot often not fully private to remove the masks when they are overcome by the heat of the outfit. The head-piece fits very close to the face and allows for only a limited air-space for breathing.
34. Lieutenant John Matthews R.N., *A Voyage to the River Sierra Leone*, London 1788, p. 136.
35. Thus Dr. J.O. Lucas, himself a Yoruba, quotes Dr. J. Abayomi-Cole approvingly as dismissing the suggestion that *Shigidi* could be sent out on an errand to kill someone at a distance, and instead, proposing that the death of the person in question may be caused by thought-protection. See J.O. Lucas, *The Religion of the Yorubas*, Lagos 1948, 364.

36. Jahnheinz Jahn, *Muntu*, London 1961, p. 130.
37. See footnote 17.
38. J. Pedersen, *Israel: Its Life and Culture*, London 1940, Vol. I–II, p. 99f.
39. *ibid.* p. 103.
40. Jahnheinz Jahn, *op. cit.* p. 100.
41. *ibid.* p. 101 f.
42. Douglas Warner, *Ghana and the New Africa*, London 1960, p. 38.
43. Bengt Sundkler, *The Christian Ministry in Africa*, 2nd Edition, London 1960, p. 307.
44. Fr. P. Tempels, *Bantu Philosophy*, Eng. Trans., Paris 1959, p. 41f. The Mende word for a founding father is *Nde-moi* or *Le-moi*, a word used for the Supreme Being.
45. J.R. Wilson-Haffenden, *The Red Men of Nigeria*, London 1930, p. 295.
46. R.W. Williamson, *Religious and Cosmic Beliefs on Central Polynesia*, London 1933, Vol. II, p. 21.
47. cp. K.A. Busia, *The Position of the Chief in the Modern Political System of Ashanti*, London 1951, p. 241.
48. R.S. Rattray, *Ashanti*, Oxford 1923, p. 215.
49. cp. W. Robertson Smith, *The Religion of the Semites*, London 1894, Lecture IX.
50. *Harvard Theological Review*, Vol. XLIV No. 3, July 1957, p. 116.
51. *Classical Quarterly*, Vol. 32, Nos. 3, 4, p. 223, Article by O. Skutch and H.J. Rose.
52. cp. Harry Sawyerr, *Sierra Leone Bulletin of Religion*, Vol. I, No. 1, 1959, Article on *Sacrificial Rituals in Sierra Leone*.
53. Jomo Kenyatta refers to the Kikuyu as Gikuyu. *See Facing Mount Kenya.* p. xv, footnote 1.
54. Jomo Kenyatta *Facing Mount Kenya*, Mercury Books, London 1961, p. 265ff.
55. cp. C. Bolaji Idowu, *Olodumare*, London 1962, p. 190.
56. Mircea Eliade, *The Myth of the Eternal Return*, Eng. Trans., Pantheon Books, New York 1952, p. 4.
57. Carl Jung, *Psychological Types, Eng. Trans.*, London 1923, p. 601.
58. Fr. P. Tempels, *op. cit.*, p. 34ff.
59. cp. P. Tempels, *op. cit.*, p. 32.
60. cp. Eva Meyerowitz, *The Sacred State of the Akan*, London 1961, pp. 54, 198.
61. cp. M.J. Field, *Search for Security*, London 1960, p. 98.
62. cp. P. Tempels, *op. cit.*, p. 85f.; See the whole of cap V. See also J. Wilson-Haffenden, *The Red Men of Nigeria, passim; Eva Meyerowitz, The Divine Kingship in Ghana and Ancient Egypt*, London 1960, pp. 27f., 61f.

ANCESTOR WORSHIP (PAGES 43–55)

1. cp K.A. Busia's story of a woman who had been ill and in a dream had been given a ball of medicine. On waking up she found the medicine

under her pillow, arranged for some of it to be dispensed to her, and she recovered. She also claimed to have preserved the remaining portion of medicine (*The Position of the Chief in the Modern System of Ashanti*, London 1958, p. 25). For a like case when a boy dreamt that his mother brought him his school fees, and later on found the money under his pillow; some years afterwards, when the boy had left school and begun to save some money, he dreamed again that his mother had come to recover her loan and he later found he had missed the equivalent sum from savings he had kept in a locked cash box, see Douglas Warner, *Ghana and the New Africa*, London 1960, p. 38.

2. cp. *International Archiv for Ethnographie*, Leiden, Band 39, 1940 p. 190, Article by S. Hofstra.

3. This prayer is culled from an unpublished document left by the late Rev. W.T. Harris, formerly a Methodist Missionary at Segbwema, Sierra Leone, who died in 1959.

4. cp. E.B. Idowu, *Olodumare*, London 1962, p. 116. For details of some of these rites, see *Sierra Leone Bulletin of Religion* Vol. I, No. 1, 1959; and Vol. II, No. 1, Articles by Harry Sawyerr on Sacrificial Rituals in Sierra Leone; African Traditional Sacrificial Rituals and Christian Worship.

5. cp. International Archiv fur Ethnographie, Band 34, 1937, p. 114, Article by S. Hofstra on *Tokpogolei*.

6. The Creoles also set a dish or dishes of rice and stew on a table overnight for a newly-deceased relative, and sometimes to assure relatives long-dead, that they are not forgotten.

7. cp. Capt. J.R. Wilson-Haffenden, *The Red Men of Nigeria*, London 1930, p. 295.

8. cp Mrs. Monica Wilson, *Communal Rituals among the Nyakusa*, London 1959, p. 162. Jomo Kenyatta, *Facing Mount Kenya*, Mercury Books, London 1961, p. 232ff.

9. cp. Monica Wilson, *op. cit.*, p. 165.

10. cp. J.V. Taylor, Primal Vision, London 1963, pp. 143 185ff. Although the Creole *hoti-hoti* aptly describes the warming effects of alcohol, yet all spiritous liquors gladden the heart.

11. E.B. Idowu, *Olodumare*, London 1962, p. 93.

12. Vol. 7, No. 1, Article on *The Sense of Concreteness in Yoruba Worship*, by T.F. Fabiyi with Harry Sawyerr.

13. E.B. Idowu, *op. cit.*, p. 69.

14. cp. *ibidem*, p. 116.

15. cp. *ibidem*, p. 192.

16. cp. Edwin Smith, *African Ideas of God*, p. 25, footnote.

17. Jomo Kenyatta, *Facing Mt. Kenya*, Mercury Books, London 1961, p. 260, but see the whole of Cap X.

18. *ibidem*, p. 232.

19. *ibidem*, p. 239.

20. *ibidem*, p. 234 f.

21. *ibidem*, p. 239.

22. Mrs. Monica Wilson, *Communal Rituals among the Nyakyusa*, London 1959, p. 162.
23. cp. *ibidem*, p. 5.
24. *ibidem*, p. 74.
25. *ibidem*, p. 77.
26. *ibidem*, p. 165 *et passim*.
27. Ulli Beier, *A Year of Sacred Festivals*, A Nigerian Magazine Production, Lagos 1959, p. 26.
28. K.A. Busia, *The Position of the Chief in the Modern Political System of Ashanti*, London 1958, p. 96.
29. R.S. Rattray, *Ashanti*, Oxford 1923, pp. 80, 125, 136; Eva Meyerowitz, *The Sacred State of the Akan*, p. 149a. cp. J.B. Danquah, *The Akan Doctrine of God*, London 1944, p. 28.
30. R.S. Rattray, *op. cit.*, p. 216.
31. *ibidem*, p. 215, footnote 3.
32. K.A. Busia, *op. cit.*, p. 31f., cp. p. 29.
33. E.B. Idowu, *op. cit.*, p. 116.
34. Jomo Kenyatta, *op. cit.*, p. 239.
35. *ibidem*, p. 236.
36. cp. *ibidem*, p. 74.
37. *ibidem*, p. 239.
38. E. Evans-Pritchard, *Neuer Religion*, London 1956, p. 119.
39. *ibidem*, p. 22.
40. *ibidem*, p. 27.
41. E.B. Idowu, *op. cit.*, p. 193.

THE AFRICAN CONCEPT OF DEATH (PAGES 56–66)

1. Jomo Kenyatta, *Facing Mount Kenya* (London: 1968), p. 234.
2. *Ibid.*, pp. 236–40.
3. J.B. Danquah, *The Akan Doctrine of God* (London, second edition, 1968), p. 156f.
4. *Ibid.*, p. 156.
5. *Ibid.*, p. 168.
6. *Ibid.*, pp. 68, 82f.
7. J.B. Danquah, *op. cit.*, p. 160.
8. E.B. Idowu, *Olodumare* (London, 1962), p. 194.
9. Idowu, *op. cit.*, p. 171ff; Harry Sawyerr, *God: Creator or Ancestor* (London, 1970), p. 83.
10. Placide Tempels, 'Bantu Philosophy', Présence Africaine (Paris, 1959), p. 73, cf. p. 72.
11. Danquah, *op. cit.*, p. 162.
12. Cf. E. Meyerowitz, 'Concepts of the Soul among the Akan of Ghana', *Africa*, Vol. XXI, 1951, p. 25 f; W.T. Harris and Harry Sawyerr, *The Springs of Mende Belief and Conduct* (London, 1968), p. 88; Idowu, *op. cit.*, p. 169.

13. cf., E.B. Idowu, *op. cit.*, p. 200; Harris and Sawyerr, *op. cit.*, p. 30 *et passim*.
14. Daryll Forde, *The Efik Traders of Calabar* (London, 1956).
15. Harris and Sawyerr, *op. cit.*, p. 32.
16. Eva Meyerowitz, *The Akan of Ghana* (London, 1958), p. 97.
17. cf. Harry Sawyerr, *Creative Evangelism* (London, 1968), pp. 24, 90; L.V. Thomas 'The Study of Death in Negro Africa', in Lalage Brown and Michael Crowther, *Proceedings of the First Congress of Africanists* (London, 1964), p. 152; Edwin Loeb, 'Tribal Initiations and Secret Societies, *American Archaeology and Ethnology*, Vol. XXV, 1929, p. 264f; Kenneth Little, *The Mende of Sierra Leone* (second edition, 1968), p. 122f; Colin Turnbull, *The Lonely African* (London, 1963), p. 131f.
18. J.R. Wilson Haffenden, *The Red Men of Nigeria* (London: 1930), p. 295 for a summary statement on this topic of Sawyerr, *op. cit.*, p. 54.
19. Weah Sawyerr and Harry Sawyerr, 'Death', *Sierra Leone Bulletin of Religion*, Vol. 5, No. 2, 1963.
20. Harry Sawyerr, *op. cit.*, p. 123.
21. Meyerowitz, *op. cit.*, pp. 55, 88.
22. cf. Note 26.
23. Chinua Achebe, *Things Fall Apart* (London: 1969), p. 70.
24. *Africa*, Vol. 38, 1968, p. 65.
25. *Ibid.*, p. 68.
26. Lalage Brown and Michael Crowther, *op. cit.*, p. 159.
27. *Ibid.*, p. 163.
28. *Ibid.*, p. 164.
29. R.S. Rattray, *Religion and Art in Ashanti* (London: 1930, reprint), pp. 159, 163.
30. *Ibid.*, p. 164.
31. Harris and Sawyerr, *op. cit.*, p. 30f.
32. cf. *Africa*, Vol. 38, p. 67.
33. cf. Harris and Sawyerr, *op. cit.*, pp. 30f, 136f; Idowu, *op. cit.*, pp. 197; Meyerowitz, *op. cit.*, p. 97.
34. Harry Sawyerr 'A Sunday Graveside Libation in Freetown after a Bereavement'. *Sierra Leone Bulletin of Religion*, Vol. 9, No. 2. It should be noticed in this account that when living members of the family are mentioned, names are introduced by others than the principal speaker.
35. Danquah, *op. cit.*, p. 120.
36. Eva Meyerowitz, *Divine Kingship in Ghana and Ancient Egypt* (London: 1960), pp. 103–5.
37. cf. Idowu, *op. cit.*, p. 173.
38. Gerald Moore, 'The Imagery of Death in Africa Poetry', *Africa*, Vol. 38, 1968, p. 68.
39. Idowu, *op. cit.*, p. 185.
40. J.H. Schlenker, *Temne Traditions, Fables* (London: 1864), pp. 25–29.
41. Harris and Sawyerr, *op. cit.*, p. 9.
42. Danquah, *op. cit.*, p. 77.
43. Idowu, *op. cit.*, p. 43f.

PSYCHE IN CONFLICT (PAGES 67-84)

1. previously unpublished.
2. William Bascomb, *The Yoruba of Southwestern Nigeria*, New York 1969, p. 71.
3. P. Amaury Talbot, *The Peoples of Southern Nigeria* 4 Vols. London 1926, Vol. 2, p. 259.
4. Harry Sawyerr, *God: Ancestor or Creator?* London 1970, p. 82.
5. K. Antubam, *Ghana's Heritage of Culture*, Leipzig 1963, pp. 39, 35, 36; of Eva Meyerowitz, *The Divine Kingship in Ghana and Ancient Egypt* London 1960, p. 104.
6. J.B. Danquah, *The Akan Doctrine of God*, Second Edition, London 1968, pp. 82, 85–88.
7. J.O. Lucas, *Religions in West Africa and Ancient Egypt*, Lagos 1970, p. 282.
8. P. Amaury Talbot, *op. cit.*, Vol. 2, p. 260.
9. *Ibidem*.
10. Antubam, *op. cit.*, pp. 93-6.
11. Christaller, *Dictionary of the Ashante and Fanti Languages* revised and enlarged by J. Schweitzer, 1933 edition, pp. 254–5.
12. J.G. Williamson, *Akan Religion and the Christian Faith, Accra 1965, p. 109.*
13. E. Meyerowitz, *Divine Kingship* in Ghana and Ancient Egypt, p. 103.
14. M.J. Field, *Religion and Medicine of the Ga People*, London 1961 Edition, p. 115.
15. Meyerowitz, *Ibidem*, p. 104.
16. M.J. Field, *Search for Security*, London 1968, p. 113.
17. H. Debrunner, *Witchcraft in Ghana*, Kumasi 1959, p. 9; cf M.J. Field. *Search for Security*, p. 36.
18. J.B. Danquah, *op. cit.*, p. 112, cf. pp. 115, 117.
19. K. Antubam, *op. cit.*, p. 40.
20. Ibidem.
21. quoted by H. Debrunner, *op. cit.*, p. 16.
22. R.S. Rattray, *Ashanti*, Oxford, 1925, p. 153.
23. cf G.J. Afolabi Ojo, *Yoruba Culture*, London and Ife 1966, p. 162, 185, 189; E.G. Parrinder, *Religion in an African City*, London 1952, pp. 14–17.
24. M.J. Field, *Search for Security*, p. 36.
25. J.O. Lucas, *Yoruba Language*, Lagos 1965 p. 145; of Harry Sawyerr, *God: Ancestor or Creator?*, p. 44.
26. E.B. Idowu, *Olodumare*, London 1962, p. 169.
27. *Ibidem*.
28. *Ibidem*, p. 171.
29. *Ibidem*, p. 172.
30. *Ibidem*, p. 173.

31. J.O. Lucas, *Yoruba Language*, p. 145.
32. K. Dickson and P. Ellingworth (ed) *Biblical Revelation and African Beliefs*, London 1969, pp. 116–136.
33. *Ibidem*, p. 121.
34. *Ibidem*, p. 122.
35. *Ibidem*.
36. K. Dickson and P.E. Ellingworth, *op. cit.*, p. 103.
37. *Ibidem*, p. 124.
38. Harry Sawyerr, *God: Ancestor or Creator?*, p. 83.
39. cf W.T. Harris and Harry Sawyerr, *The Springs of Mende Belief and Conduct*, Freetown and London, 1968, pp. 60–68, 113.
40. Karl Laman, *The Kongo*, Uppsala 1953.
    George W. Harley, *Native African Medicine*, New Impression London, 1970.
    M.J. Field, *Religion and Medicine of the Ga People*, London 1937;
    Michael Gelfand *Medicine and Custom in Africa*, Edinburgh and London, 1964.
    Thomas Winterbottom. *An Account of the Native Africans in the Neighbourhood of Sierra Leone.* 2 Vols. London 1803, 2nd Edition 1969, p. 200.
41. Monica Wilson, *Rituals of Kingship among the Nyakyusa*, London, 1957, p. 115.
42. Mary Douglas, *Purity and Danger*, London, Second Impression 1969, p. 155.
43. P. Amaury Talbot, *op. cit.*, Vol. 3, p. 717.
44. *Ibidem*, p. 716.
45. H.A. Junod, *The Life of a South African Tribe*, 2 Vols, New York 1962, Vol. 1, p. 191.
46. M.J. Field, *Religion and Medicine of the Ga People*, p. 115.
47. Monica Wilson, *op. cit.*, p. 185.
48. N.A. Fadipe, *The Sociology of the Yoruba* Ibadan 1970, p. 279, cf. p. 129.
49. John Middleton, *Ingbara Religion: Ritual and Authority among an East African People*, London 1960, p. 44.
50. *Sudan Notes* Vol. L, 1969 p. 50f, Article by Evans-Pritchard on Zande Notes about Death, Soul and Ghost.
51. cf. W.T. Harris and Harry Sawyerr, *op. cit.*, p. 68, 72 f.
52. Ruth Finnegan, *Survey of the Limba People of Northern Sierra Leone*, London 1965, p. 121.
53. cf. Harry Sawyerr, *Creative Evangelism*, London 1968 pp. 30–32. W.T. Harris and Harry Sawyerr, *Tohalei op. cit.*, pp. 68–73.
54. Monica Wilson, *Rituals of Kinship among the Nyakyusu*, pp. 186–189.
55. W.T. Harris and Harry Sawyerr, *op. cit.*, p. 109 and Appendix V.
56. J.O. Lucas, *Religions of West Africa and Ancient Egypt*, p. 319.
57. *Ibidem*, p. 318.

58. Daryll Forde, *African Worlds*. Seventh Impression, London 1970, p. 73, Essay by J.D. and E.J. Krige on *The Lovedu of the Transvaal*.
59. Fr. Martin Jarrett-Kerr, *African Pulse*, London 1961 Edition, p. 36.
60. Monica Wilson, *Communal Rituals of the Nyakyusa*, London 1959, p. 152.
61. W.T. Harris and Harry Sawyerr, *op. cit.*, p. 22.
62. G.W. Harley, *op. cit.*, pp. 250–253. cf Martin Jarrett-Kerr, *op. cit.*, p. 33.
63. J.O. Lucas, *Religions in West Africa and Egypt*, p. 320.
64. W.T. Harris and Harry Sawyerr, *op. cit.*, p. 68.
65. Quoted by G.W. Harley, *op. cit.*, p. 197.
66. Meyer Fortes, *Oedipus and Iob, in West African Religion*, Cambridge, 1959. See especially, p. 53.
    C.G. Baeta, *Christianity in Tropical Africa*, London 1968, p. 182,
    J.V. Taylor, *Primal Vision*, London 1963, pp. 174,ff.
67. C.G. Baeta, *op. cit.*, p. 182.
68. *Ibidem*, p. 189.
69. *Ibidem*, p. 184.
70. *Ibidem*, p. 189.
71. *Ibidem*, p. 188.
72. Monica Wilson, *Communal Rituals of the Nyakyusa* p. 161; *Rituals of Kingship among the Nyakyusa*, p. 233; *Religion and Transformation*, Cambridge 1971, pp. 33, 39.
73. J.V. Taylor, *op. cit.*, p. 177.
74. *Ibidem*. p. 180.
75. Henry McKeating, *Living with Guilt*, London, 1970, p. 21.
76. G.W. Harley, *op. cit.*, p. 39.
77. Claude Levi-Strauss, *The Savage Mind*, E.T. London 1966, p. 221.
78. Fr. Martin Jarrett-Kerr, *op. cit.* p. 121.
79. K. Dickson and P. Ellingworth, *op. cit.* p. 125 cf. Harry Sawyerr, Creative Evangelism, p. 137ff; W.T. Harris and Harry Sawyerr, *op. cit.*, p. 20 ff.
80. Monica Wilson, *Rituals of Kinship among the Nyakyusa*, pp. 180–189. Harry Sawyerr *Creative Evangelism* pp. 30–32.
81. P. Amaury Talbot, *op. cit.* Vol. 2, p. ?
    Thomas Winterbottom, *op. cit.*, Vol. 2, p. 200.
82. Mary Douglas, *The Lele of Kasai*; London 19??, p. 123.
83. Karl Laman, *op. cit.* Vol. II, p. 64.
84. *Ibidem* p. 33f.
    When cohabiting the man and woman 'both lie on their side' (p. 34).
85. *Ibidem*.
86. Monica Wilson *Communal Rituals of the Nyakyusa*, p. 165.
87. Evans-Pritchard, *Nuer Religion*, London 1956, p. 275.
88. Monica Wilson, *Communal Rituals of the Nyakyusa*, p. 145.
89. *Research Review*, University of Ghana. Institute of African Studies, Vol. 3, No. 1, 1966, pp. 78–81, Article by A.C. Denteh on Birth Rites of the Akan.

90. Africa Vol. VI, 1933, p. 38; but see the whole Article on Azande Blood-Covenants.

Some of the words the blood is supposed to have heard include the following:

'May the blood untwist from you with respect to . . .'
(the special case being named).

WHAT IS AFRICAN THEOLOGY? (PAGES 85–99)

1. C.G. Baeta (ed.) *Christianity in Tropical Africa*, London 1968 p. 436. Essay on The Predicament of the Church in Africa.
2. *ibidem*, p. 426.
3. ibidem, p. 427.
4. E.B. Idowu, *Towards an Indigenous Church*, London 1965.
5. C.G. Baeta, *op. cit.*, p. 427.
6. W.G. de Lara Wilson, *Christianity and Native Rites*, London 1960, p. 6.
7. *ibidem*, p. 14.
8. *ibidem*, p. 15ff.
9. J.F. Ajayi, *Christian Mission in Nigeria, 1841–1891*, The Making of a New Elite, London 1965, p. 235.
10. *ibidem*, p. 225 and note 4.
11. Edward Blyden, *Christianity, Islam and the Negro Race*, (African Heritage Books I, 1967 Reprint, Edinburgh), p. 68.
12. *ibidem*, p. 66.
13. *ibidem*, p. 281.
14. *ibidem*, pp. 280, 281.
15. T.E. Beetham, *Christianity and the New Africa*, London 1967, p. 45.
16. *ibidem*, p. 46.
17. *The Church in Changing Africa*, J.N.C. New York. 1959. p. 68ff.
18. *ibidem*, p. 69.
19. *ibidem*, p. 23.
20. *ibidem*, p. 5.
21. D.B. Barrett, *Schism and Renewal*, London and Nairobi 1968, p. 78 Table II (Statistics of Independency Adherents in Thirty-Four African Nations 1967).
22. *ibidem*, Chapter VIII.
23. *ibidem*, p. 95.
24. Harold W. Turner, African Independent Church, 2 vols. Vol. II, Oxford 1967, p. 32.
25. *ibidem*, p. 326.
26. *ibidem*, p. 319.
27. *ibidem*, p. 326.
28. *Drumbeats from Kampala*, London 1963 pp. 32ff, 54.
29. cp. Notes 1–4.
30. *Drumbeats from Kampala*, p. 38.

31. Th. Müller-Kruger, in *South East Asia Journal of Theology* Vol. 6, No. 3, pp. 59–73.
32. *Orita* Vol. II No. 2, December, 1968, p. 68. Article on *Understanding African Religion.*
33. H.W. Turner *op. cit.*, p. 337f.
34. *ibidem*, p. 347.
35. *ibidem*, p. 346.
36. Mia Brandel-Syrier, *Black Woman in Search for God*, London 1962, p. 149.
37. H.W. Turner, *op. cit.*, p. 339.
38. *ibidem*, p. 352.
39. *ibidem*, p. 353.
40. *ibidem*, p. 360. For a study of separatist Churches in East Africa, the reader is referred to F.B. Welbourn and B.A. Ogot, *A Place to Feel at Home*, London 1966 especially Chapters 11 and 12.
41. F.B. Welbourn, *East Africa Christian*, London 1965, p. 42.
42. C.G. Baeta, *op. cit.*
43. Raime Harjula, Preparatory Paper for the Theological Conference for Africa sponsored by the Lutheran World Federation at Makumira, Tanzania. July 15–22, 1970, p. 5.
44. Bengt Sundkler, *The Christian Ministry in Africa*, Uppsala 1960, p. 280ff. but see the whole of Chapter 6.
45. C.G. Baeta, *op. cit.*, pp. 183–194.
46. *ibidem*, p. 184f.
47. cf. G.C. Oosthuizen, *Christianity in Africa*, London 1968, p. 207.
48. Mia Brandel-Syrier, *op. cit.*, p. 158.
49. F.B. Welbourn, *op. cit.*, p. 41.
50. H.W. Turner, *op. cit.*, p. 370ff.
51. cf. Harry Sawyerr, *Creative Evangelism*, London 1968, cap 2, 3.
52. *Lambeth Essays on Ministry*, London 1958, p. 69.
53. *ibidem*, p. 58.
54. James H. Cone, *Black Theology and Black Power*, New York, 1969, p. 50.
55. *ibidem*, p. 147.
56. *ibidem*, p. 148.
57. As demonstrated in a political map of Africa drawn up by the cartographer of the Department of Geography of Fourah Bay College (1968).
58. F.B. Welbourn and B.A. Ogot, *A Place to Feel at Home*, London 1966, p. 132.
59. cf. Jack Mendelsohn, *God, Allah and Juju* (Religion in Africa Today) New York 1962, Chapters V and VI.
60. In this connection, African theologians must eschew making global statements like those of Edward Blyden, cp. *Christianity, Islam and the Negro Race*, Edinburgh University Press 1967 reprint, Cap 6 and John Mbiti, *Concepts of God in Africa*, London 1970. The latter is an A–Z presentation of the various tribes known to the writer and therefore inaccurate in many instances.

THE BASIS OF A THEOLOGY FOR AFRICA
(PAGES 100–110)

1. London 1960.
2. M. Eliade, *The Myth of the Eternal Return*, New York 1957, p. 92.
3. Ibid p. 141.
4. E.B. Idowu, *Olodumare: God in Yoruba Belief*, London 1962, chapter 10.
5. Eva Meyerowitz, *The sacred State of the Akan*, London 1951, p. 121; also Margaret Field, *Search for Security*, Evanston 1960.
6. cp. Norman Pittenger, *The Word Incarnate*, New York 1959, p. 17.
7. Paul Fueter, *Theological Education in Africa*, in IRM 1956, p. 395.
8. *op. cit.*, p. 306.
9. Meyerowitz, *op. cit.*, pp. 65-8.
10. Janheinz Jahn, *Muntu*, New York 1961, p. 131.
11. See Jomo Kenyatta, *Facing Mount Kenya*, London 1938, p. 131.
12. See Alec Vidler, *Christian Belief*, London 1950, p. 111ff.
13. *Christianity and African Culture*, Accra 1955, p. 51. cp. Kenyatta *op. cit.*, p. 231.
14. See especially Mircea Eliade, *The Myth of the Eternal Return and Patterns in Comparative Religion*, London 1958.
15. See K. Busia in *African Worlds*, edited by D. Forde, London 1954.
16. See J.R. Wilson-Haffenden, *The Red Men of Nigeria*, London 1930, p. 295, and E. Meyerowitz, *op. cit.*, chapter 10.
17. M. Field, *op. cit.*, p. 48; Kenyatta, *op. cit.*, p. 233, and S. Nadel, *Nupe Religion*, London 1954, p. 13.
18. Freetown, Watic Press 1949, p. 64.
19. Quoted by G.K.A. Bell in *Christianity and World Order*, Harmondsworth 1940, p. 87.
20. See M. Field, *op. cit.*, chapter 4; Meyerowitz, *op. cit.*, chapter 10, and Idowu, *op. cit.*, p. 9 and chapter 9.
21. See Idowu, *op. cit.*, chapters 9 and 10; Harru Sawyerr, *Sacrificial Rituals in Sierra Leone* and *Traditional Sacrificial Rituals and Christian Worship*, in *Sierra Leone Bulletin of Religion* 1959(1) and 1960(2).
22. See the essay by A.G. Herbert in *Ways of Worship* by Edwall, Hyman and Maxwell, London 1952, p. 77.

SOTERIOLOGY VIEWED FROM THE AFRICAN SITUATION (PAGES 111–123)

1. Leonard Hodgson, *The Doctrine of the Atonement*, London 1951, p. 60 cf. P.T. Forsythe, *The Work of Christ*, London 1938, cap IV.
2. G. Milligan, *St Paul's Epistles to the Thessalonians*, London 1908, p. 78f.
3. Th. C. Vriezen, *An Outline of Old Testament Theology*, Oxford 1958 (Eng. Trans.) p. 202.

4. *ibidem*, p. 172.
5. Margaret Field, *Search for Security*, London 1960, p. 36.
6. Eva Meyerowitz, *The Divine Kingship in Ghana and Ancient Egypt*, London 1960, p. 104; cf. Africa 1952, Article on Concept of the Soul among the Akan.
   H. Debrunner, *Witchcraft in Ghana*, Kumasi 1959, Chapter 3.
7. Eva Meyerowitz, *The Akan of Ghana*, London 1958, p. 47.
8. J.B. Danquah, *The Akan Doctrine of God*, Second edition, London 1968, pp. 68, 82f., 94f.
9. H. Debrunner, *op. cit.,*, p. 16.
10. J.B. Danquah, *op. cit.,*, p. 86f.
11. S.G. Williamson, *Akan Religion and the Christian Faith*, Accra 1965, p. 141.
12. J.C. Carothers, *The Psychology of Mau Mau*, Nairobi 1954, p. 13; cp. Placide Tempels, *Bantu Philosophy*, Eng. Trans., Paris, p. 30ff.
13. cf. W.T. Harris and Harry Sawyerr, *The Springs of Mende Belief and Conduct*, Freetown 1968, p. 81.
14. Chinua Achebe, *Things Fall Apart*, London 1967 edition, p. 24.
15. *ibidem*.
16. *ibidem*, p. 26ff.
17. *ibidem*, p. 112f, 118.
18. *ibidem*, Chapters 21–25 see especially p. 186.
19. Sylvia Leith-Ross, *African Woman*, London 1939, p. 100.
20. cf. Colin Turnbull, *The Lonely African*, London 1965, p. 211.
21. L. Levy-Bruhl, *The 'Soul' of the Primitive*, (Eng. Trans.) London 1928 (1965 edition), p. 341 cf. p. 211ff.
22. S. Gelfand, *Medicine and Custom in Africa*, Edinburgh and London 1964 p. 107 but see the whole of Chapter 8.
23. A.R. Radcliffe-Brown and Daryll Forde, *African Systems of Kinship and Marriage*, London 1930, p. 105.
24. W.T. Harris and Harry Sawyerr, *op. cit.,*, p. 97.
25. See Note 16.
26. G.T. Basdem, *Among the Ibos of Nigeria*, London 1966 edition, p. 229 cf. J.V. Taylor, *Primal Vision*, London 1963, p. 182.
27. cf. E.B. Idowa, *Olodumare*, London 1962, Cap 13;
    J.B. Danquah, *op. cit.,*, pp. 68, 82f., 94ff.;
    G.T. Basdem, *op. cit.,*, p. 230;
    Harry Sawyerr, *God: Ancestor or Creator?* London 1970, p. 83;
    Eva Meyerowitz, *The Akan of Ghana*, p. 97;
    The Divine Kingship in Ghana and Ancient Egypt, p. 123.
28. Harry Sawyerr, *God: Ancestor or Creator?* London 1970, p. 83.
29. Daryll Forde, *African Worlds*, London 1954, p. 204.
30. Jacob Drachler (ed.) African Heritage, New York 1963 p. 148;
    Daryll Forde, *op. cit.,*, pp. 191–196;
    (cf. Placide Tempels, *op. cit.,*, p. 65ff;
    C.G. Baeta (ed.) *Christianity in Tropical Africa*, London 1968, p. 310.
31. W.T. Harris and Harry Sawyerr, *op. cit.,*, p. 96ff.

32. Daryll Forde, *op. cit.*, p. 204.
33. Monica Wilson, *Religion and the Transformation of Society*, London 1971, p. 38.
34. H. Debrunner *op. cit.*, Chapter 6.
35. J.V. Taylor, *op. cit.*, pp. 175–177;
    C.G. Baeta (ed.) *op. cit.*, Chapter 8.
36. C.G. Baeta, *op. cit.*, p. 130.
37. Alexander Hetherwick, *The Gospel and the African*, Edinburgh 1932, p. 111f.
38. John Middleton, *Lugbara Religion*, London 1960, p. 22f.
39. C.G. Baeta, *Prophetism in Ghana*, London 1962, p. 60.
40. *ibidem*, p. 65.

CHRISTIAN EVANGELISTIC STRATEGY IN WEST AFRICA (PAGES 124–132)

1. Jessie Page: *The Black Bishop, Samuel Adjayi Crowther* (London, 1910), p. 5. *Orisha* is the generic term for a Yoruba divinity other than God.
2. D.A.C. Crowther: *The Niger Delta Pastorate*, 1864–1892 (London, 1896), p. 193f.
3. ibidem, p. 76f.
4. *ibidem*, p. 10.
5. *ibidem*, p. 9.
6. *ibidem*, p. 20.
7. *ibidem*, p. 85.
8. *ibidem*, p. 11f. J.C. Taylor also refers to sacrifices offered to *Tshi*, a god supposed to preserve the Ibos from harm, especially from witchcraft, and to sacrificial rites performed on a feast day, *Guo alà* (sacrifice for the land). See Crowther and Taylor: *The Gospel on the Banks of the Niger, I* (London, 1859), pp. 348, 368, and cp. 287, 376.
9. See C.G. Baëta: *Prophetism in Ghana* (London, 1962), pp. 37, 52, 86, 102.
10. See E.B. Idowu: *Olodumare* (London, 1962), p. 116.
11. *ibid.*, p. 123.
12. D.A.C. Crowther, *op. cit.*, p. 180.
13. For instances of similar considerations facing Indians in the seventeenth century, see Lucien Levy-Bruhl: *The Soul of the Primitive* (London, 1928), p. 308ff.
14. Dr. C.G. Baëta boldly states that 'we live with our dead'. See *Christianity and African Culture* (Accra: Gold Coast United Christian Council, 1955), p. 60.
15. See Ulli Beier, *A Year of Sacred Festivals in a Yoruba Town* (Lagos: Nigeria Magazine Publications, 3rd edn., 1959), p. 26.
16. E.B. Idowu, *op. cit.*, p. 193, on the *Egungun*.
17. See 'The Selfhood of the Church in Africa', *Ministry* (Morija, Basutoland), Vol. III, no. 4 (July 1963), pp. 151–8.

18. Blyden always boasted that 'the African, like the Israelite, is not a hero-worshipper' (see *Proceeding at the Banquet in Honour of E.W. Blyden, LL.D.,* Sierra Leone, 1907, p. 21). He was unfortunately unfamiliar with the native customs prevalent around him in Sierra Leone and other parts of West Africa.

19. cp. E.O. James: *Sacrifice and Sacrament* (London, 1962), p. 233: 'All the deepest emotions, experiences and evaluations of human beings in every state of culture and in all religions find expression in actions, objects and external rites believed to be the vehicles conveying spiritual benefits to the recipients, so that "inward" and "outward" experience meet in a higher unity.'